F.A.T.C.A.T.

**FELINE AUDIO TELECOMMUNICATING
CRIMINAL APPREHENSION TEAM**

DAVID D. FELTY

Library of Congress Control Number: 2020922172

HARDBACK: 978-1-953791-31-3
PAPERBACK: 978-1-953791-30-6
EBOOK: 978-1-953791-32-0

Ordering Information:

For orders and inquiries, please contact:
1-888-404-1388
www.goldtouchpress.com
book.orders@goldtouchpress.com

Printed in the United States of America

F.A.T.C.A.T. SUMMARY

Can felines become crime fighters? Dogs, yes! But cats? A twelve year old, Teddy, and a private investigator, Ross, decide to find out. After two years of intense observation and dedicated effort, they develop a gadget that when worn by the cats, enable them to communicate with humans. Ross, Teddy and the feline audio telecommunicating criminal apprehension team, F.A.T.C.A.T., set out to show their value and prove they can while pursuing the culprits in four mysteries.

Teddy is on summer vacation, juggling his grass cutting jobs and keeping in touch with new neighbor, Miss Leona, who his mother has designated as his "go to" while she works. Teddy chooses to think of her as his contact. Then there's summer football practice where an unfriendly teammate complicates things while Teddy tries to secure the position of running back. Most of all he helps Ross care for and work with the cats.

Teddy is missing his dad, a Special Forces military man who is regularly sent on top secret assignments. He is usually gone for a week, maybe a month or two, but this time he has been gone for ten months. Teddy and his mom will not give up hope. They pray and trust that God will bring him safely home.

Receivers

Speaker

Microphone

BL

BIOGRAPHY FOR DAVID D. FELTY

David D. Felty has enjoyed working with children for many years, starting as a church youth director and Sunday school teacher. After a stint in the armed forces he returned to college where he earned a degree in Business Education. He became a high school business teacher, but quickly realized his passion lay in elementary education. It was while teaching third grade that he found his love for telling, and writing stories.

David has written many short stories for children and published with *Highlights For Children*, *Guideposts magazine* and picture books entitled *With Those Hands, Bobby Bumblebee's Big Ego Boost and Harrigon – A Dragon's Tale*.

It is his desire, through his writing, to help children learn moral values, good manners, and a loving, caring nature that will enhance their trip through lives journey.

F.A.T.C.A.T.

My first chapter book

For

Dale Kimon Felty

My first born son

With whom I enjoyed many firsts

CONTENTS

F.A.T.C.A.T.
Feline Audio Telecommunicating Criminal Apprehension Team
By David D. Felty

CHAPTER ONE
BONNETS, HELMETS, HATS

I knew the F.A.T.C.A.T. was there, but the shadows hid their four small figures. They were totally unseen and unheard.

Bobbie Lee screamed out in the biggest voice she could muster, "Hands above your head, face the wall, you're surrounded!"

Billie Rose came on the telecommunicator to Ross, "We've got him, HURRY!"

Ross came on saying, "Let's go Teddy, I'll deal with Bones. I'm coming down the alley, almost there. Take care of the cats. I'll see you later at the house.

"You got it, Boss," I responded in my excitement.

I saw Ross run up to Bones, who had just managed to unlock the door. He clamped on the cuffs calling out, "Good job, kitties."

"I'm not a kitty, I'm a cat!" exclaimed M&M. "Me too!" chimed in Moon Sun.

"Okay, whatever, SORRY! You kitt…eh, I mean cats, did great," said Ross.

"Theodore Bartholomew Tessleman, what are you doing? It is almost time to go."

came the rather disappointed voice of my mom.

I jumped off the bed where I was sitting. I'd been thinking of the success of F.A.T.C.A.T.'s first case.

I didn't like it when my mom used my full name. It always meant she was upset with me. Everyone calls me Teddy, normally, like the president, Teddy Roosevelt. My dad had a high regard for the 26th president. I don't know why he wanted to name me that and Bartholomew from the bible, one of the apostles. Jesus told Bartholomew, also called Nathanael, that in him there was no deceit.

So, my dad told me he wanted me to be honest and to treat everyone with love and respect just like I would want to be treated. I sometimes have a problem with that, especially with some of the kids, but I try. I touched Dad's face in the picture I had been holding. I said, "I miss you Dad, I love you, Be safe."

I finished getting ready and hurried to the kitchen where mom was waiting patiently. "Sorry Teddy, but you know I don't like to be late," she said.

After Pastor Bill's sermon I headed for my Sunday School Class. I stopped short as I walked into my classroom. Apparently some tall white-haired lady in blue was substituting. She wore a blue jacket over a blue sweater with a blue beaded necklace, a blue skirt and blue shoes. She almost blended into the blue wall behind her.

Fine, I thought. *All this blue fits my mood perfectly.* I already felt bad after the service. I always go with Mom, but, most of the other kids were with both their moms and dads. My dad is gone and we have no idea where he is or when-or even if-he will return. He is a military man in Special Forces. Everything he does is top secret. We never know where he is going or when he is coming back. He tells us as much as he can. He always says, "Don't worry. I'll be fine." But, this time he has been gone for ten long months. I'm twelve years old. Two months is forever.

On top of that Ross, our usual teacher, was not there. Ross is a dectective with the M.P.D. Ross was always at Sunday school ready to teach. Something very important must have come up for him to miss.

I work with Ross. I love working with him and the cats. Cats you might ask? Dogs in police work, yeah, but cats? Yes CATs.

The lady in blue opened the attendance book and began calling the roll since she didn't know us like Ross did. Even if you weren't looking at her you could tell she was smiling from the sound of her voice.

"Teddy Tessleman."

"That's me," I called out as I held up my hand and looked in her direction.

She was smiling as she said, "Well Teddy, Ross has told me a little about you. He says you help him out with his cats, or felines, as he prefers to call them."

If she only knew how much I help Ross with the cats she would be shocked. But, for now, only Ross, me, and Mom knew about the F.A.T.C.A.T.

I love to talk about cats, but Miss Leona, that's her name, needed to get into the lesson. She called the names of the other ten kids and then began, The half hour passed quickly and the lesson helped my sadness. She taught from the story of the prodigal son. His father was very happy to see his son after he had been gone for so long. There was a big celebration. It made me think how wonderful it will be when my dad finally comes home.

As I left the church building, and started my two-block walk home, the heavy black clouds overhead opened up and down came the rain. The cool raindrops felt good as I began to hum the tune my dad used to sing when we were caught in a shower, called "Raindrops Keep Falling On My Head."

When I got home I noticed that Ross's car was in his driveway. As I walked into the house my mom said, "Oh, my, Teddy, you're soaked. Go put on dry clothes, and then go see Ross. He left a message saying he needs to talk to you right away."

I felt a wave of excitement. Sunday school and, I guess, the showers had "washed away" my sad tears. I couldn't wait to hear what Ross had to say.

We had been working on a way to use the cats to help in his work. Ross is a genius, the smartest person I know. He and I invented a way to communicate with his cats, or felines. We started two years ago right after my dad left on a military assignment.

Because of my dad's job we have moved a lot. That's why I couldn't have a cat of my own though I love them more than any other animal. I've wanted a cat as long as I can remember but Dad always said we didn't need the extra baggage. Anyway, I noticed when we moved here two years ago that Ross had cats, four of them, so I went over to ask if he would let me see them.

"Of course, you are welcome to visit with them whenever you want." He seemed to be glad for the possible help.

I often wondered what the cats might be saying to each other as they jumped and romped and chased each other around the house.

"What do you think they are saying, Ross?" "That's an interesting question, Teddy."

That's when we got the idea to start recording the sounds the cats made and observe the actions that went with them. The days passed and our recordings grew until we had over 500 of the 800 meows and mews that cats make, matched to words. Then Ross, with my help, started working on a device that would transmit a word for a sound and a sound for a word. Two years went by before we perfected the device so the cats could wear it. The cats were trained to push one of two buttons that would allow their sounds to be heard as words from a small speaker, or transmitted to earbuds worn by me and Ross. The words spoken by us were translated and transmitted to the cats in their sounds. Then came the design for the speaker and transmitter that were small enough for the cats to wear and powerful enough to be easily heard. IT WORKED!

We call the device F.A.T., not fat as in blubber, but F period, A period, T period. It stands for Feline Audio Telecommunicating. And, C.A.T. which stands for Criminal Apprehension Team.

I entered the house to find Ross and the cats. He had put the devices on the cats. They were seated on stools around the kitchen table.

"Teddy, are you ready for some excitement?" asked Ross.

"Oh wow, this is what we've been waiting for! Are we ready C.A.T.?" I called out as I took a seat at the table.

"Yes of course, by all means, without a doubt, are you kidding, is my tail missing, is my dad's name Moon, get out of town, is it raining outside, is Boss Ross the best detective in the world, get with the program," was the jumbled response from four very excited cats.

"Simmer down, simmer down," Ross said as he stood up and began to explain the case he had been working on and had decided to bring the F.A.T.C.A.T. in on for a first trial run.

There had been a series of robberies from jewelry stores in neighboring towns. Ross had reason to believe that our town, Midtown, might be next. It seemed that the robberies all happened on Mondays. If police were stationed in the area the thief would probably get spooked off. Our goal was to use the cats where regular police might not work. The F.A.T.C.A.T. would be perfect. They could hide in small places in the alley without being seen. Was all the time we'd spent observing, listening, recording and working to put this gadget together going to pay off? Would the cats behave, pay attention, be interested? Now was the time to find out.

Midtown only had two jewelry stores. One of them kept diamonds, ice, pretty shiny sparkly stones. That's what the thief was after. Ross had discovered that most of the robberies took place shortly after dark. The suspect's name was Bones, a fugitive on the most–wanted list.

We made our plan. I was to wait at the alley entrance that led to the back of Glimtone's Gemstones, the possible crime site. My job was to transport the cats in a basket on my bike and take them safely home later. Ross would deal with Bones.

After we had discussed the plan, Ross asked me to take off the devices and hang them on the pegs on the wall under each cat's name.

"Let's take off your devices," I said to the cats.

Bobbie Lee, a blondish tiger stripe with only a knob for a tail rang out, "You mean bonnets. I don't like the name devices."

"Yeah," agreed Billie Rose, her sister, who was gray with a nice tail.

"Baloney," disagreed M&M, which was short for Midnight Marauder. M&M was a gray and black tiger stripe, large and very handsome. We call him Big M a lot because he is such a large cat.

"Helmets, that's what they are," exclaimed Moon Sun, a fluffy black cat, as he stormed around like a bull charging a red cape.

I calmly said, "Okay, I'll call them HATS, you call them what you will, helmets, bonnets, whatever. When I say let's put on our hats, girls get bonnets, boys get helmets."

It was late afternoon when I went home. I told Mom about feeling so sad earlier in the day. "Mom, do you think Dad will ever come home?"

She said, "We can never give up hope, Teddy. We'll just stay here until we know." That evening when I was ready to go to bed I got on my knees. I knew that my heart-felt prayers could do wonderful things. I think that's in the book of James. I heard it in Sunday school one time. So, I prayed for my dad, wherever he was. I prayed for the success of our first attempt to use the F.A.T.C.A.T. to catch a criminal. Thoughts and questions kept rolling over in my mind. Have we done enough training with the cats? Would the devices work when a real crime was happening? Would the cats really be interested? Again, would they behave? On and on it went until I finally fell asleep.

Morning came with the dense fog that sometimes follows a rain after a dry spell. After breakfast I went over to Ross's house to check on the cats. They were fine. All in a comfy place snoozing. The afternoon was misery. I tried to read, watch TV, play a game on the computer, Nothing seemed to ease my jitters.

Evening finally arrived. I went to get the cats ready. "Okay cats, let's get your hats on."

After I put Bobbie Lee's hat on she pushed the button that enabled her to communicate. I had put my receiver on my belt and my headset was in place so I could talk to them.

Bobbie Lee said with much concern, "I don't like the name – hat!" "Oh," I accepted her complaint.

By then I had put Billie Rose's hat on. "Me neither! It's not a good name," she agreed. Moon Sun's hat went on and he agreed with the girls.

Then on went M&M's. "It's perfectly clear, they should be called helmets." Then back and forth it went.

"That's crazy, they're bonnets!" "Of course, bonnets!"

"Helmets is the name!" "No question, helmets!"

"Bonnets!" "Helmets!" "Bonnets!" "Helmets!" "Stop!" I demanded as I turned my receiver off.

"I thought we already settled this. Girls - it's bonnets, boys – it's helmets, me – it's hats."

At that point Ross came in and no one said another word.

Final instructions were given and we were off. I rode my bike with a basket full of the F.A.T.C.A.T., and Ross drove his car. His car was like a regular police car, but it was unmarked.

Ross parked just down from the alley entrance on Weeping Willow Boulevard. I stopped just inside the alley where I could see the back entrance to the jewelry store. One by one the cats jumped out of the basket. They were a strange sight with their bonnet- helmet-hats on as they cautiously made their way down the littered alley finding things to hide behind. I hid myself.

On dry runs we had stressed the importance of silence, and staying still. But we had two boys and they seemed to always want to find a better vantage point after we were set. I don't know how many times we said, "Find your spot and stay put."

It would be much harder for a couple of big policemen to stay out of sight than a small cat. Had Ross been doing this on his own he would have waited inside the building and nabbed Bones when he entered. However, that had been tried in other areas with no success. It seemed that Bones had a sixth sense when it came to police. Now it was F.A.T.C.A.T.'s time to try.

The sun was going down and everything was making long shadows. After a short time a tall, slender, downright skinny man came slinking up the alley to Glimtone's Gemstones. His key and a big bag for the loot were all he carried. He looked carefully to the right, then left. When he seemed satisfied he was all alone, he took out the key and inserted it in the lock.

"CLICK"

CHAPTER TWO
BONES

Bobby Lee's voice rang out. Bones dropped his loot bag as his arms flew into the air. Obviously he had been caught completely off guard. He looked around for the source of the voice as Ross ran up to him slapping on the shackles.

Ross read Bones his rights and gave him some advice. Maybe he should not have, but Ross was serious about trying to get these bad guys to turn their lives around.

As he escorted Bones to his car he said, "Stop stealing. Begin using your hands for honest work and then give generously to others in need. That's God's way. Try it!"

I chuckled as one by one four small figures leaped into the basket on my bike. "Bobbie Lee present and accounted for," said the excited little cat.

The rest followed, "Billie Rose ready to roll." "Moon Sun on board."

"Let's go Teddy, I'm hungry," said M&M in a voice he tried to make bigger than all the rest.

This gave me an idea I would run by Ross later.

With a few woohoos and yeehaws we left the crime scene and took off down Weeping Willow Boulevard on the bright red bike my dad got me for my twelfth birthday just before he left on assignment. I knew he would be proud of the part I was playing in the F.A.T.C.A.T. project. He believed strongly in God and country. He wanted people to be free and safe to express themselves and live a godly life. He would be happy I'm working with Ross, who is like my dad in many ways.

For months Ross and I had been sold on the usefulness of the cats wearing their F.A.T.

– Feline Audio Telecommunicators working as a team to apprehend criminals – Criminal Apprehend Team, which we call F.A.T.C.A.T. And now we had our first success.

I continued to pump hard as I took out my cell phone to call my mom.

"Mom we're on our way in, Umpf!" My bike hit a crater sized hole I didn't see and I almost dropped my phone. I held on to it and kept control of my bike, but caught a little flack from my passengers.

"Watch it, Teddy! Let's get home in one piece, okay?"

I saw a couple of people looking at us from the sidewalk and realized that Big M had pushed the lid up from the basket and was peering out.

"This just might be the scariest part of the whole adventure," he complained to the other cats.

I got back to my mom who sounded a little fearful for us herself.

"Mom, we did it. Bones is on his way to lock-up. Would you get things ready? The cats deserve a real treat. Order extra anchovies, big ones!"

"Yes Teddy, of course I will, but pay attention to what you're doing. Get home safe.

I'll take care of everything on this end," pleaded my concerned mom.

I soon rounded the corner of Weeping Willow Boulevard and rode into Ross's driveway at 505 Birchwood Drive. The cats enjoyed the ride home. That is except one. Big M was still a little rattled about the hole I had hit.

"Okay, cats, let's get in the house, take off our hats, and get comfortable. My mom will be here in a little bit with some vittles," I announced.

"Fine, fine, I need nourishment. I am very discombobulated, Teddy," said Big M.

"Discombob….what? What in the world is that, M&M?" I asked.

I had never in my twelve years heard a word like that, let alone from a cat. These cats never ceased to amaze me, especially the intelligence of Big M.

"Well cats, that bony brute's ice heisting days are over, thanks to you," I complimented them.

Bobbie Lee chimed in, "Yeah, he won't dump any more diamonds into his big black loot bag."

I laughed and muttered, "That's amazing, Bobby Lee."

At that moment Ross walked in the door. He said, "Speaking of amazing, you're all amazing."

Then my mom came in and the aroma of pizza supreme with anchovies filled the air.

M&M already had his eye on the biggest anchovy on the pizza. "Let's eat!" his voice rang out. I removed his helmet and he dug in.

I hardly remember my head hitting the pillow when I awoke to the sound of voices outside. Mom had told me there would be a new neighbor in the small house just east of us. It had been empty for a while.

The young couple that lived there were starting a family, as Mom put it. I thought if you had a mom and dad, brothers and sisters, grandmas and grandpas and so on, you had a family. She meant they were going to have a baby, two of them in fact. Twins, wow, how neat is that? I've always thought that twins were cool. I had a twin in my class this year. There was only one of them because they usually separate them at school for some reason. They didn't look alike, though. The one in my class was Mike. The one in another class was Mika.

"Careful, I don't know if we can get this piano up the steps and in the door," came a very concerned voice.

Another voice responded, "Sure we can, slow and easy, I measured it. We have two inches to spare. That's an inch on each side."

I couldn't stand it any longer. I jumped out of bed glancing at the clock. It was 8:00 a.m. Mom had let me sleep in. After the exciting success, and our pizza party last night, I guess I was tired.

Today I needed to check on the cats and take care of their needs. Then, I had a yard to cut after lunch. Ross wanted me to meet him at 3:00 p.m. to discuss our new case. Maybe I could help the new neighbor.

I looked out the window. To my surprise standing on the front porch was Miss Leona.

She wasn't the blue lady today. She wore a red sweatshirt and jeans.

Mom had told me that the new neighbor lady would be my contact, the person to go to if I had needs. I guess it's good if it makes Mom feel better, but why would she think I need a contact? It's not like she's part of our team or anything.

Miss Leona! That's cool! I liked her last Sunday as a substitute Sunday School teacher.

I got dressed and fixed the cereal Mom had left on the table along with a note.

Teddy,

Miss Leona is moving in next door today. Go over and see if there is anything you can do to help. I didn't tell you who it was going to be. I thought it would be a nice surprise. She will take care of your lunch. She's looking forward to being there for you.

Love you,

I spent the morning helping Miss Leona move boxes to the rooms she wanted them in. As we talked, I discovered she had just retired from teaching. She had lived in an apartment in town but had decided to move into a small house on the edge of town. She was going to work from her home tutoring and giving piano lessons, and, of course, keeping tabs on me. I was okay with that since it made Mom feel better.

My dad loved to play piano. He had taught me a little. Funny for a tough Special Forces guy like him to play the piano, but he said it was relaxing. Maybe I'd take lessons from my new neighbor and surprise him when he got home?

As I carried the last of the boxes into the kitchen Miss Leona said, "Hope you like PB&J. Sorry, but I'm not set up to make much of a meal yet."

"Oh, that's great, thank you. I was wondering if maybe you could give me lessons when you get settled, if it's okay with my mom."

"Yes, Teddy, Tess already talked to me about it. She was hoping you'd like to. Maybe we could trade. I'll give you and Tess piano lessons. And, you can cut my grass."

"Alright, it's a deal!" I agreed.

I left Miss Leona's house around 2:00 p.m. and headed for Ross's to check on the cats. As I went in I heard a considerable amount of meowing and cat sounds. What was the big discussion all about?

I checked food and water and cleaned their boxes. Then I started to put their hats on so they would be ready when Ross got there, and possibly clue me in on what all the chatter had been about. I caught Bobbie Lee in mid-word as I put her bonnet on.

"Meoten up, the boss is coming."

Ross walked in looking extra excited, "Okay team, get a load of this!"

F.A.T.C.A.T.

CHAPTER THREE
SQUEAK, CLATTER, PUTT-PUTT

Ross had asked me to meet him to discuss yesterday's success. He had a serious look on his face along with his excitement. I wasn't sure if he was angry, frustrated, or just anxious.

He slipped on his receiver/transmitter (RT), and said, "I'm not convinced if what we have here is for real yet. Was it a fluke; just dumb luck on our part?"

"That's crazy," me and four cats disagreed.

Ross conceded, "Yes, maybe, but nonetheless, we're going to do it again and again until I'm convinced."

Then Ross grabbed a bottle of water from the fridge, took a big swig and settled on his favorite recliner chair and said, "Okay, listen up."

The cats sat down and he started, "Bobbie Lee, Billie Rose, Moon Sun, M&M, and Teddy. My C.A.T., you may be the best thing to happen to law enforcement since Sherlock Holmes. And, this may be just the beginning! It seems we have a barrage of missing pets here in Midtown. It's got to be petnapping. At last report there were 20 missing pets. Chief Edding asked me to assist in the case and maybe even apprehend who is behind this caper.

"Let's roll!" came a quartet of kitty voices.

But I said, "Ross, our cats need a bigger sounding voice."

"What do you mean, Teddy? Do you want them to sound like dogs, big dogs?"

"No, I want them to sound like bears. Growly voices, scary voices, something that will make bad guys shiver in their boots."

Ross thought, shook his head the way he does, and said, "Well Teddy, you just might have something. But, problem is, it is going to cost a lot of money to develop and integrate into our system. I'm tapped out, my friend, drained, flat busted. We've soaked a small fortune into this project."

"I'll help. I can get some more lawns to mow," I offered.

"No, Teddy. Thanks, that's great of you. I might have gone through everything I had, but I don't owe anyone anything. I'll float a loan. Maybe it won't cost all that much, and if we're successful the Chief will make F.A.T.C.A.T., with our assistance, a part of the MPD with a big salary. Let's go for it."

"Okay, great, but don't forget I'll help with the cost if you need it." "Thanks, Teddy."

Ross continued to talk about the assignment. It seemed that most of the pets were disappearing from the upper northeast side of the city.

When Moon Sun heard this he spoke up. "I want to go see my dad, Moon. He lives in that area. He prowls his neighborhood every night. If anything suspicious has been going on, he will know about it."

"Excellent, Moon Sun," Ross approved. "Teddy, let's make it happen. Check in with your mom. If we can, we'll try to find Moon this evening."

The time had flown by. It was 6:00 p.m. At home I found Mom busy cooking.

"Oh good, Teddy, I was about to call you. Miss Leona is going to join us for dinner." "Great, we can talk about piano lessons, but I need to be gone this evening for an hour or so around 7:30. It's official detective business.

"Okay, I know Ross will look out for you. But, you be careful anyway."

"Sure, Mom, I'll put on my armor like the knights of old, or maybe coach will let me wear my football gear."

"Very funny, Teddy, but you can put on the full armor of God. Remember you told me a couple weeks ago how Ross taught your Sunday school class about the armor of God.

It's protection against the devil. Remember you're not just trying to catch the bad guys, but you're also fighting the one who influences them."

"Yes Mom, you're right. I'll be careful and I'm in good hands."

I made a good arrangement with Miss Leona to cut her grass for piano lessons. She was thrilled. Mom was pleased and said she wanted us to be able to play something for Dad when he came home. I didn't realize that Mom and Miss Leona were so well acquainted. They were in the same Sunday school class and Mom had handled the real estate deal when Miss Leona bought the house next door. As we talked, I noticed something very interesting on the front page of the newspaper laying on the table.

Rewards were being offered for the missing pets!!

I jumped up from the table. "May I be excused, please? Gotta go! Great meal! Thanks, Miss Leona," I said as I ran out with the paper in my hand. I knocked on Ross's door.

"Ross, did you see this? Rewards are being offered for the return of missing pets, several of them, some for a big bunch of money. Maybe that could pay for our cat's big voices!"

"Yes, I saw it. That just might suggest a motive for our petnapper's activities too."

We got the F.A.T.C.A.T. ready and headed out. Moon lived and prowled the night away about eight blocks north of us.

The quiet spring night was filled with the lilac smell. Moon Sun disappeared into the darkness where he found his dad in the thicket he liked to hang out in. Moon was close enough to his son that his sounds were translated over Moon Sun's telecommunicator.

"Stay in the shadows. It's not safe. Animals are disappearing. I've seen two men in an old rusty truck moving slowly down Lilac Street several times most evenings. I think they are grabbing them."

Suddenly the stillness of the night was broken. I heard a squeak, clatter, and putt-putt, as an old rusty truck slowly crept by where I was waiting on my bike. The sweet smell of lilacs was killed by smoky, smelly exhaust. I thought Ross ought to pick them up for polluting.

I heard Moon say, "Stay low, don't move, that's them."

The rusty old truck passed and Moon Sun came back and reported to Ross. "Alright, I've got an idea," Ross said.

Ross had this way of moving his head side to side and shaking it as if to say "yes" when he was getting an idea. Kind of like a bobble-head.

"Okay team, I've got a plan," Ross said after a few seconds of head bobbing.

The words had hardly passed his lips when squeak, clatter, and putt-putt, the beat up truck went slowly by again.

The F.A.T.C.A.T. all mewed, "Quick, Boss, follow that truck!"

Ross took off, expecting to see the taillights of the old truck around the corner, but there was nothing. They had vanished. Not a sign, not a smell, not a sound.

Ross was obviously thinking hard as we returned home. "See you tomorrow, he said. "Same place, same time."

The next morning I would be starting summer football practice for the Junior High team. My summer was full. I was working with Ross and the F.A.T.C.A.T., I knew we'd be developing the bigger voice for the cats, cutting grass, taking piano lessons, and going to football practice. Piano and football were new very important things. My dad would be happy if he knew I was going to play football on a real organized football team. It would please him that Mom and I were learning to play piano. I enjoy both, but mostly I want Dad to be proud of me.

I went straight to bed. Morning arrived with the pleasant voice of my mom, "Rise and shine, Sunshine, I'd like to have breakfast with you before I leave for work."

The aroma of Mom's coffee, the sweet smell of flapjacks and maple syrup, and an inviting whiff of fresh sausage paddies invited me into the kitchen. After a nice conversation with Mom and a good breakfast, I headed for the door.

"Thanks Mom, that was great. I'm stuffed."

"You're welcome. I enjoyed having breakfast with my favorite fellow. It seems like one of us is always in a rush. Good luck with football practice," replied Mom.

Lockers were assigned. Equipment was passed out. I talked to my friends that I've played back lot football with and met some of the other guys. It was going to be neat to be on a real team with a coach.

The coach barked out some instructions, "Get on your gear and go to the practice field, boys. We'll try to get organized for a winning season."

I suited up and was making my way to the field when I saw Sam Edding quickly approaching. Apparently he was going to try out his shoulder pads on me before we got to the practice field. Just as he lowered his shoulders to collide with me from the side I jumped backward causing him to miss and go sprawling on the ground. I'm not sure if maybe my foot might have assisted his going down. Like I said earlier, I sometimes have a problem with the actions of crazy kids. Looking up and offering a silent, sorry. I walked over to offer him a hand. Why would he want to flatten me?

"Hey Sam, you might want to wait for practice to begin," I suggested. "Remember, we're on the same team."

He jumped to his feet and took off. I'm sure he was hoping that nobody saw his near- miss. Sam is a bit bigger than me. If he had connected, I would have been the one on the ground. Was he just trying to be tough? I wasn't worried about him. I know how to take care of myself. After all, my dad is a warrior and my good friend is a detective I also know that being tough doesn't mean you can't have a soft side, like dad playing piano and Ross loving kitties, like me. Picking on people doesn't mean you're tough. And playing piano and liking cats doesn't make you weak. Did he think I was an easy target? What was his problem? I didn't know Sam well. Just knew him by name when I saw him. He seemed angry. Did I do something to make him want to flatten me? I decided that I would get to know this guy and find out his problem.

Practice started and ended and I was on my way to my days work and an evening of surveillance.

Now that Miss Leona was my new neighbor, Mom had given me instructions to check in with her during the day when she wasn't going to be home. She was going to be my "contact," not babysitter. She was going to fix lunch and be there if I needed anything. I knew that made Mom feel better about having to be gone all day some of the time. It took some pressure off her.

"How was practice, Teddy?" Miss Leona asked as she placed a sandwich beside the bowl of soup she had waiting for me on her new kitchen table.

The room looked different than when I helped carry boxes around. There were interesting pictures on the walls. Everything was put away and it was spic and span. The pleasant smell of the food made me realize how hungry I was.

"Practice was great. I think the coach is going to try me in a running back position.

One of the guys who played in the backfield last year moved away. I'm a fast runner, and move around pretty good. You know, bob and weave, side step, stuff like that," I said as I munched on the sandwich. After a few bites I said, "I'd like to cut your grass after lunch, Miss Leona, if that's okay with you."

"Yes, Teddy, that will be fine. Would you like to begin your piano lessons this week?" "Sure, let me know when you have a spot in the afternoon. Football practice is in the morning. Late afternoons and early evenings I will spend with Ross on our new case and a project we are working on. I'll have grass to cut most afternoons."

"Okay Teddy, come in after you finish the grass and we'll see where we need to start.

We will set a time. You do realize you'll need to find some time for piano practice as well," she informed me.

I like being busy. I'm getting swamped, but I really like everything I'm doing, so it doesn't seem like it. I remember from another Sunday school lesson hearing, "Work hard with enthusiasm at whatever you do, just as though you were working for the Lord." I do. I even whistle while I work. I even sing sometimes if I don't think anybody can hear. I once sang to the cats. They thought it sounded funny. They laughed. It sounded funny to hear them laugh.

I love the smell of fresh-cut grass. The whirr of the engine and the grass smell filled the air as I made laps around Miss Leona's yard. It was nothing like last night when we watched the old rusty truck make its noisy, smelly appearance and disappearance. I was curious and eager to find out if it would make another appearance this evening.

After cutting the grass I went in to show Miss Leona how far along I was in learning to play the piano. When she heard me play a little song dad taught me, she said, "You're coming along nicely. I think we can start in the second or third book."

We set the time of Nine O'clock on Saturday morning for my lessons and I was off to check on the cats.

I'd forgotten that Thursday was Ross's short day at work. I walked in just as Bobbie Lee launched herself from a perch on top of a thing Ross got for the cats to climb up and on and into. Ross was resting in his favorite chair. He had been working on a diagram for the new piece we would create to give the cats bigger voices.

Whomp! Smack dab on Ross's chest.

"Ouch, Bobbie Lee, you rascal, that hurt! You're small but mighty, aren't you?" an alarmed Ross cried out.

Then he turned to me, "Hey, Teddy, good to see you. I don't think she wants me to get any rest. I've been working on your idea. It shouldn't be too difficult or expensive. I think we can modify their transmitters much like bad guys can disguise their voices on a phone. Of course smallness is the issue. Therein lies the challenge. But, we can do it. If you want, we can get started."

"Yes, for sure, let's get on it," I said.

I reached down and picked up Bobbie Lee. She looked like she was laughing.

Ross said, "I checked with your mom to see if you could hang out and discuss our project and new case before we go out on surveillance this evening. I'm fixing a pizza." Big M meowed what I was sure was a question. Probably asking about anchovies.

Ross looked at me and grinned. He thought the same thing.

He laughingly said to Big M, "And, yes, I have anchovies on it just for you."

Big M licked his chops. I think they are beginning to understand our words without their hats on.

The table was set for six. Ross and me and.....

F.A.T.C.A.T.

CHAPTER FOUR
PETS IN NETS

Four cats sat on their stools along the two sides of the table. Each had a plate with an anchovy cut into small pieces so they could easily eat it.

Ross and I sat at the ends. Together we were a C.A.T. The cats deserved special treatment because they were so important. They were the F.A.T.C.A.T. Without them we would not be a team.

Pizza gone, anchovies gone, we were ready to discuss the Big Voice project. Big M jumped down from his stool, walked into the living room, and jumped on Ross's chair. He rolled over on his back and settled down for a catnap. Billie Rose and Bobbie Lee sat on their stools licking their paws and washing their faces. Moon Sun disappeared. He had probably followed M&M's lead and found a good place to take a snooze.

Ross showed me a gadget that could be attached to a phone to change the sound of voices. He took it apart and pointed out the part that caused the change.

"We will need to reduce the size of this and integrate it into our system. We'll have to modify the tone until we produce the sound desired. This is not a problem.

I felt somewhat puzzled. "If you say so, Boss. Growly voices, a sound that will make the bad guys shiver in their boots," I reminded him.

"You got it, Teddy. Our cats will sound like Tigers. Let's get the tigers ready to go. I hate to interrupt M&M's handsome rest but time is marching on. I'd like to be in place before it gets dark."

We rounded them up and put their hats on with very little comment. I think they were finally accepting the Hat-Bonnet-Helmet thing.

Ross said, "I'd like for all of us to go in my car this time. We are just going to wait and watch to see if that rusty old truck appears again. If it does, we will try to find out where it goes. I don't want whoever is driving to know we're watching. If they are truly our suspects, next time we will try my plan."

Ross drove to the spot on Lilac Street where we first saw them. Me and the cats sat in the back of Ross's black car. It was surprisingly roomy for a small sporty car. But this part of the team is not very big.

Big M broke the silence. "Sure beats a basket with a lid on it, and ride's much better also."

"Yeah Teddy, why don't we always travel this way?" asked Moon Sun. "Gotta be sixteen to drive a vehicle, cats," I answered.

"What's that got to do with anything?" Billie and Bobbie chimed in.

"Never mind, girls, just know that when the action starts, the bike carts," I answered.

"Oh," "Really?" "Don't understand that!" "Balderdash and poppycock!" came a barrage of disagreement.

"Whatever. You cats are something else!"

"Yes, I know, we're tigers," Moon Sun said, giggling.

BANG!! Came a big backfire, clatter, clatter, squeak, putt-putt, from right outside the window of the car. I hit my head on the ceiling and all four cats scrambled for the floor and under the front seats.

"Okay team," Ross said. "Here we go. Stay alert! Let's not lose them again." "We didn't lose them, Boss, you did," said Big M.

"Right you are, don't want that to happen again," Ross agreed. "Here we go. Eyes open."

Ross started slowly down Lilac Street with lights off. There wasn't any traffic so following them shouldn't be a problem. They rounded the corner. Ross turned his lights on and rounded the corner to find nothing, not a thing in sight. How could a small, old, slow moving, noisy, smelly truck just disappear?

Four cats were speechless, I was speechless, even Ross was speechless. This was strange, this was totally weird.

Ross finally spoke up, "Okay, tomorrow we try my plan."

His head was bobbing. I knew he was seriously frustrated as we scoured the neighborhood for any sign of that mysterious old truck. After ten or fifteen minutes we headed back to Ross's house. I helped to remove the hats from the cats and went home.

Mom was sitting in the living room reading a book. "Glad you're home, Teddy. Fresh baked cookies over there if you'd like a snack," she offered.

"Thanks, we've had a disappointing evening. Something good would be nice. Do you believe a noisy, stinky, ole truck can just disappear into thin air?" I asked.

"Mercy, Teddy, that sounds crazy. How could that happen?"

"That's the question for sure," I answered as I took a big bite out of a fresh chocolate chip cookie still warm from the oven.

Mom invited me to watch an hour of TV with her. It was a crime drama series that we both enjoyed watching occasionally. In this episode they used a fake delivery of a very valuable work of art the criminals wanted as bait to draw them out. It worked. This gave me an idea, and I couldn't wait to tell Ross. I wouldn't see him until the next day. How could I sleep?

Morning came. I had slept after all. With breakfast done I headed for football practice.

Approaching the locker room I saw Sam waiting. He held out his hand. I thought he wanted to shake and apologize.

As I offered my hand, he slapped it and said, "Watch your back, Teddy Bear! You're going down. Get used to the taste of dirt, Tessleman!"

I couldn't think of a good response so I just said, "Go for it."

My first impulse was to whomp him up side the head, but I knew that wasn't right. I usually ask myself, "What would Jesus do?" Then there's the rule, Do unto others as you would have them do to you. It's hard to be kind to someone who wants to do you bodily harm but I knew God would help me with this problem. His word says, "Love your enemies! Do good to them!" I know that's right, but I can only handle so much of this nonsense before I lose my cool. What's up with this guy anyway?

Practice went okay. We ran the length of the field four times. I was happy to come in first every time. But in blocking practice I just happened to be teamed up with you-know- who. I held my own, but I must admit he flattened me a couple of times. I was back on my feet in a flash and was ready for more.

In passing and receiving, I was sent out to receive. I caught some really bad passes by either speeding up a lot or diving for them.

Dirt, yes, I ate some dirt, but it wasn't because of Sam.

After practice the coach called me into his office. He said, "Teddy, I'd like you to fill a backfield spot. I see a lot of potential. You have hustle and you have good hands. And most of all, I like your attitude. Think about it. If you want it, it's yours. By the way, don't let Sam get to you. He has some issues he's working through. It isn't you he's mad at. He's just lashing out. I'll talk to him. He's going to be a good lineman if he can get it together."

"Thanks, Coach, I don't need to think about it. I want the spot."

I had two yards to cut on Friday afternoon. I had hoped that the F.A.T.C.A.T. would be on the case Friday evening, but Ross had a "calling all cars" emergency, one that he wasn't free to discuss with his Junior Detective. I hoped we could return to the case soon. I was eager to tell Ross my idea. After all, according to a brief phone conversation with Ross, five more pets had disappeared. I wished I could be more a part of the crime investigation and law enforcement thing. But I realized that JDs were just interested in learning about it to decide if it's a career we might want to go for.

Ross started the club about a year ago. It had to be August because you have to be twelve to join. I turned twelve on August 13, last summer. In about two weeks I'll be thirteen.

I fed the cats and made sure they had water. Then, I decided to take a ride on my own. I rode the eight blocks to the spot on Lilac Street where we last saw the rusty old truck. In circling the block I noticed an old abandoned service station on the corner of Hemlock and 9th Streets. The pumps had been removed, and just the shell of the building remained. The windows in the back portion of the building had been painted over. Why would anyone do that? Good question. Could someone have something to hide? Outside there were empty oil drums setting around. I was curious, but didn't try to get inside. That was a job for Ross. I thought I heard a dog bark. Perhaps a guard dog, but why would anyone store anything in that old building? *Curious, yes very curious*, I thought.

All evening, I wished Ross was available. I hated not being able to go right after the petnappers. The trail was hot and I didn't want it to cool off.

I was still a bit frustrated as Saturday arrived. It was quickly offset with the very pleasant smell of cinnamon rolls. I opened my eyes and Mom had set a plate with a huge roll on my chest. She stood there grinning as I took the plate and sat up.

"Whoa, what's this?"

"Breakfast in bed for my favorite fella. Take your time, but remember you have a piano lesson at 9:00."

I devoured the roll and drank the glass of milk she had set on my bedstand.

Mom had encouraged me to keep Saturday mornings open so we could spend some time together. Her job, at least for now, gave her week-ends off. My piano lesson was scheduled for Saturday morning at 9:00 a.m. That was fine because Mom is in about the same place as I am and she'd decided to take lessons with me. We are thinking that when Dad comes home he will be surprised and pleased that we are both learning to play. We are going to learn a duet especially for the occasion. I won't allow myself to think he's not coming back, and I don't want Mom to do that either.

If he's lost or held captive out there somewhere, he'll get free and come back to us. No question about it. We'll never give up hope.

We rang the doorbell. Miss Leona came to the door in jeans and a sweat shirt. Her hair was up in curlers. I wasn't sure what they were. Mom never uses them. She had slippers on her feet and a piece of toast in her hand.

"So sorry, guys, I overslept. I never do that. This retirement business is hard to get used to. If I was still teaching I would have been grading a pile of papers by now," she explained. "Let's get started. I'm so happy to help you two learn more about playing piano."

Miss Leona went to get the books she wanted to start us in. I took a seat at the piano.

She looked nothing like the Miss Leona I first met. I am glad she moved in and is there if I need her during the day when Mom's gone. During this tough time it's great to be surrounded with wonderful people. Mom, Miss Leona, Ross, Coach, most of my customers whose lawns I mow. I don't think about missing dad as much.

Then, there's the cats. They are not people, but now that I can communicate with them, it's amazing the conversations we have. They don't always look at things the way people do. Are they stimulating? Are they cheerful and exciting? Yes they are. Most of the time they are very entertaining. Cats know a lot of stuff. They have their opinions. They do things in their own time. However, they do have a sense of closeness and teamwork. They all seem to be into the F.A.T.C.A.T. project. I don't know if it's because of their devotion to Ross or if they just find it fun to do something different.

Ross once told me that Big M was raised by a college professor friend of his and thought he was human until he was brought to live with him and his cats. Big M picked up a lot from his first owner. Sometimes he puts on airs. He got his name M&M or Midnight Marauder because he used to always want to roam outdoors late at night.

"C, middle C. Pay attention, Teddy, I think you're daydreaming," Miss Leona told me. "Sorry, I was. I'm back."

The rest of the lesson went well and Mom and I spent the rest of the day doing fun stuff. She did drag me along while she did a little shopping. Part of it was for me, so I guess I needed to go. We had lunch, and stopped at Midtown's small zoo. They have a tiger I enjoyed watching. Mostly I paid attention to his growl. I wondered why he let out a big growl. Maybe he did it for me so I'd know what I wanted the cats to sound like.

After we got home I kept checking to see if Ross had gotten home yet, so I could run over and share my idea with him. We watched a neat video later and I decided to call it a day.

I woke up looking forward to church and Sunday school. I was glad Ross was there. He taught more about the armor of god. He has taught about each piece of armor, from the helmet to today's lesson about the footwear. He mentioned the special protective shoes worn by the Roman soldiers and those worn by the infantrymen with spikes. He said they were much like golfers and football players wear.

I always walk the two blocks home after Sunday school, and comfortable shoes do make a difference. I know that's not what it's all about, but I enjoy my little walk home. I find it a peaceful time to think. It helps to bring me peace of mind, helps me think straight. I thought more about the idea I wanted to share with Ross.

That afternoon after lunch I was to meet with Ross. We needed to discuss our next attempt to find the old rusty truck. It's time to try Ross's plan and hopefully my idea.

About the time I got home Mom drove into the driveway. She hurried in the house to check on the lunch she had put in the crockpot to cook while we were at church. It sure smelled good, and made my mouth water. Then there was apple pie that she baked early this morning.

"It's ready, Teddy. Hope you like it," called Mom.

I took a bite and gave Mom a big smile, "Great, Mom, couldn't be better, chicken and noodles, and apple pie. Is that an all-American meal or what? Hope Dad is having something good. Guess I just hope he's having something," I added.

Mom rubbed my curly hair and whispered, "Me too."

A tear run down her cheek. I couldn't bring myself to say anything more. I just reached out for a hug.

After lunch I headed for my meeting with Ross. I wanted to tell him about the TV program I watched where they used bait to bring out the bad guys. "Hey Ross, how about using bait to get the petnappers to stop?" I asked before I even had the door shut.

"You're reading my mind, Teddy. Meet Mr. Bait here." Ross pointed a finger in Big M's direction. "I'm thinking if we leave M&M on the corner under the streetlight where he will be clearly visible they won't be able to resist."

"Yes, and put his nice blue collar on so they will know he belongs to someone. What they won't know is that his collar is a transmitter so he can tell us where he is," I added.

"You got it, Teddy. I'm going to make a detective out of you yet," Ross said as he patted me on the shoulder.

"I try, Boss, I try. Any chance we can try our plan this evening? It might be a good time. It's the weekend. The petnappers might be out."

"Why not? Everything's ready. We have bait. Maybe if they're out, they'll bite. We'll go around 7:00," agreed Ross.

I went home and spent a little more time with my mom. We practiced the piano lesson.

We finished pretty close to 7:00.

Mom made a suggestion. "Teddy, how about me riding along with you this evening?

I'd really like to know how all this works."

"Well, it's alright with me. We just have to stay out of sight after we've put out the bait. There is a small park in the middle of the block, where we can hide and watch."

Ross parked in the park also. He could see the corner from where he was. Mom and I, Moon Sun, Bobbie Lee, and Billie Rose sat behind some bushes watching. M&M sat under the streetlight where he was clearly visible.

Squeak, clatter, putt-putt came the rusty old truck. It stopped a short distance from M&M. A tall thin bald man and a short stout curly-headed man got out of the truck.

One looked at the other saying, "Nice!" "Yes, very nice!" said the other.

Slowly, quietly they approached M&M, walking as though they were out for an evening stroll. As they came near M&M, the short, stout, curly-headed man, who had been walking with his hands behind his back, suddenly produced a large net.

F. A. T. C. A. T.

CHAPTER FIVE
FROM PET TAKING TO LOCK BREAKING

Moon Sun talked to Ross over his telecommunicater, "They got Big M!"

Ross headed for the truck, ready to make an arrest. "Come out of the truck with your hands up!" he commanded.

No one was there.

"Load up C.A.T.!" I shouted.

With the cats snug in their basket Mom and I pedaled through the neighborhood while Ross drove around. The petnappers were nowhere to be found. We knew they had to be close. They had left their old truck and disappeared.

We returned to the park and waited for M&M to contact us. Soon his voice came over his collar transmitter.

"I've been put in a cage. It smells of oil. The windows are painted over. There are other pets here. Come and get me, Boss and Teddy. I don't like it here, and neither do any of the others. They want to go home."

M&M's collar transmitter was a great aid, but it didn't allow us to communicate back to him. Perhaps that would be another project down the road.

When I heard Big M's information, I was sure I knew where he was. I remembered the painted windows and the oil drums.

"I think I know where they are. I saw an old service station on the corner of 9th street. The alley goes behind it. That would explain how they get out of sight so quickly," I said.

The cats and Ross all echoed, "That's it!"

Ross drove around to the front of the building. Mom and I stayed hidden close by. Bobbie Lee, Billie Rose, and Moon Sun went in the alley behind the building just as the two men came out the back door. The cats walked slowly down the alley.

"Look! Those are nice cats. What are they wearing on their heads? They have to belong to someone. We can get at least one of them," the thin man said.

Just as they got close with their big net raised, ready to scoop up one or more cats, Moon Sun turned and said, "Stop! Drop that net, and raise your hands. You are under arrest."

The two men looked at each other. "Did that cat say that?"

From behind them Ross said, "No! We just made it look that way for shock appeal.

I'm Detective DuBoss, and yes, you're under arrest."

He read them their rights, handcuffed them, and walked them back to his car.

Ross said, "I know you have stolen these pets so you can return them if a reward is offered. Then you pretend to be doing a good thing by finding and returning the pet for the reward. The reward you wanted is not the reward you should be looking for. And, you will never collect "that" reward if you continue on the path you're traveling."

The petnappers, who were going to get the rusty old truck, left the building unlocked. We were able to enter. The room was dimly lit. I never disliked the smell of oil until then. We could see well enough to find our kitty, yes kitty. M&M didn't care what we called him because he was so glad to see us.

He showed it, too. "I am rapturous, blissful, pleased as punch, to see you, Teddy. And Tess, how wonderful of you to help out. Now, get me out of this cage!"

There were at least two dozen other pets there. I'm sure they all wanted the same thing as M&M, but they would have to wait for the right people to arrive and return them to their homes.

I saw two parrots that kept saying, "Go to the farm, go to the farm."

Ross later discovered that the petnappers lived on a farm where they had stashed other bigger animals they took. They must have said when they left the station, "Let's go to the farm," enough times that the parrots picked up on it.

For a moment I thought maybe we should try using parrots to catch criminals. Naaa, just wouldn't be as much fun. Cats are such special creatures. And, we are the C.A.T.!

Mom was on her cell ordering pizza. "Extra anchovies," she emphasized. We loaded up the basket, and headed home.

A huge grin covered Mom's face when the pizza deliveryman arrived. She had really got caught up in the evening's activity. It was good. Now she would understand better what Ross and I did, and why I felt so strongly about the Junior Detective program. In the past she just thought I was playing with Ross's cats and doing detective stuff for the JD program.

As Mom set the pizzas on the table, Big M jumped up on his stool licking his chops. Tuffs of his long fur stuck out in different directions from under his helmet. We put it on after his rescue so we could talk to him. He looked as though he had been a bit smooshed in the basket on the ride home. Ordinarily I think he would have made space for himself, but he probably enjoyed the closeness for a change. I was surprised we hadn't heard a remark or two from him. He was quieter than usual.

I asked him, "You okay, Big M?"

"Sure, Teddy." is all he said, I found that to be very unusual.

"Come on M&M, something is bothering you. You're hungry as usual, but you always have more to say than that. What's bothering you?" I asked.

"Well, I was a little scared. I don't like to admit it, but when I saw all those other cats and dogs there in the cages away from their homes and loved ones, I realized how much I love you guys. I was just so glad and consoled when you came and got me out of that vexing cage. I don't ever want to get separated like that again. I'm glad I could play a part in the capture of those two bad guys but, I may not be as brave as you all think I am."

"Oh hush up and eat an anchovy," Bobbie Lee and Billie Rose both interrupted. "We can't believe you said almost all that in words we could understand."

Then all the cats said together, "We love you too, Big M!"

I'm sure I glimpsed a smile on M&M's face as he began to nibble on an anchovy.

Mom said, "Pizza's getting cold, kitties. Oh sorry, cats, or better yet, C.A.T. Why don't we get you comfortable and remove your hats so you can eat more easily."

"Helmets!" "Bonnets!"

"Thank you Tess, good idea," all the cats said.

At that moment the door opened and the boss arrived.

"You need to have a heart to heart with your Midnight Marauder. He may have a surprising story for you. But, right now let's celebrate. Let's eat pizza," I announced.

"Yeah, anchovy, anchovy, anchovy, anchoow, meooow," as the hats came off and the anchovies went in.

We ate and celebrated like the happy criminal apprehension team we were. Another crime solved. That was two in one week.

Ross said, "If you felines keep this up I might be convinced that the F.A.T.C.A.T. can get the job done."

He told us of the farm and the animals there and a little about a possible new case. He had spoken to the Chief on the phone, but would discuss the matter on Monday.

Belly full, M&M was sound asleep on his back in the boss's chair. Bobbie Lee and Billie Rose were chasing a ball around the house, Moon Sun was still on his stool taking in every word Ross said. He seemed interested even though I don't think he understood without his helmet on.

It was getting late. Ross told me we would meet tomorrow evening after he had talked with the Chief, and also there would be a Junior Detective meeting on Wednesday.

"Special meeting, you have got to be there," he said.

My mind was like a whirlwind. I couldn't get the events of the evening to quit playing over and over - the two petnappers, Big M, our celebration, the news about the farm, the possible next case, the special Junior Detective meeting. Special? Why? Most of all the possible new case Ross had briefly shared. Someone was breaking locks on the doors of businesses in Midtown, even some homes. The weird thing was whoever was doing it wasn't going in, at least nothing had been reported missing.

I was tired, so tired. I told Mom good night, and lay down. My mind still replayed things. Broken locks, and not going in, or nothing taken, broken locks, nothing taken, bro

k en l o c z z z z z z z z

CHAPTER SIX

PERFORMANCE IS THE KEY

I awoke with a note on my chest. It said, "I love you, Teddy. Remember:

Football practice at 9:00 a.m.
Lunch with Miss Leona (Stir food in slow cooker at noon, please)
Grass to cut in the p.m.
Dinner with Mom at 6:00 (Please give the slow cooker another stir around 3)
Meeting with Ross at 7:00 p.m.

I should be home around six. I have a busy day. Miss Leona will be here just in case.

We're having some of your favorites, along with rice pudding.

I can't wait to hear what Ross has to say about your new case!

Later,
Love you, Teddy,
Mom"

I plopped a couple pieces of bread in the toaster and got out the peanut butter, jelly and milk. After I put entirely too much stuff on my toast, I went outside on the deck to enjoy my breakfast.

One of the last things Dad did before he left on assignment was put out bird feeders. Mom had filled them. The squirrels were helping themselves. We didn't care. It was so humorous to hear them complain when we interrupted them robbing the birds of their treats. They were small pine squirrels that seemed to like chasing each other.

I ate my toast and drank my milk while listening to the squirrels jabber jabber. I wondered what they were saying. Maybe I didn't want to know. I started jabbering back and they ran away.

 A few sparrows came to feed after the squirrels left. They didn't seem to mind me. Maybe they liked me being there because the squirrels went away and they could eat in peace with me kind of watching out for them a little. There's a song we sing in church: "His eye is on the sparrow, so I know he watches me." I like that. My earthly father is not around to watch me, but my heavenly Father keeps an eye on me. That's comforting.

I hoped he would keep an eye on me today. It was my first day to practice in the running back position. I wanted to do a good job. I was curious about how Sam would like blocking for me since up until now he had just wanted to knock me around. Now he would have to knock somebody else around so I could pick up yardage. Maybe he'd get the team spirit and remember he and I are on the same team.

Maybe Coach's talk helped with his anger issue. I did hear that he was angry about losing his dad, a fireman, who had died fighting a fire. Someone said Sam has been struggling ever since. I wish he didn't feel he had to take it out physically on others, and, why me? I don't know why I didn't know about this, but I didn't and now I understand why he's depressed and angry. At least I have the hope of getting my dad back. I just hope and pray somehow I will find a way to help Sam.

I rode to school and suited up. The coach called us together on the practice field. The smell of fresh-cut grass reminded me of my afternoon's work, but right now I needed to keep my mind on football.

Coach went through his "tentative first string roster," as he called it. He said, "Now boys, this is the way I see it right now. But that doesn't mean it will stay this way. If you want to stay on the first team, you'll have to prove you can do the job. Performance is the key." That's what Ross says to the cats. "If you want to be the F.A.T.C.A.T., you've got to be able to do the job. Performance is the key."

Then the coach called off the names of the boys he had chosen to fill the various positions, "Teddy Tessleman – running back, Sam Edding – right guard." And, on through the list he went.

I looked at Sam. I couldn't tell if his grin was for real when our eyes met, or if it was suggesting, "Okay Tessleman, I can make you or break you." I wanted to remind him again about the team thing. We are teammates, not opponents. Time would tell, I guess.

Our colors are white and grey. The coach divided us into two groups and said, "You boys put on the grey jerseys and this group put on white. I want to see how you handle yourselves in an actual game-type situation."

We had only learned a few plays, but enough to have a little scrimmage so the coach could see what we could do. The first play was a pass to left end. My job was to fake a handoff and then block. Then on the second play I actually took a handoff and was to go through a hole Sam was supposed to make for me. He flattened one man and moved another out of the way. I made good yardage.

Coming back to the huddle, Sam raised his hand for a high five and said, "Good job, Tessleman." I considered this a step in the right direction. Maybe the teamwork, as we practiced, would make a way for me to get to know him better.

I hesitated, but responded with, "Way to move the opposition around, thanks, Sam."

When the huddle broke for the next play, he slapped me on the shoulder pad and said, "Go for it, Tiger!"

It was Tiger, not Teddy Bear.

We had a good practice. I thought Sam and I would both keep our positions. I left feeling good.

Lunch was good too. Miss Leona was her usual cheerful self. She had been painting her living room, and there was a spot of paint on the end of her nose.

"Getting a little close to your work there, aren't you?" I touched the end of my nose and pointed to hers.

She caught her reflection in the window of the door and laughed. "I love painting.

That surely will not be all I'll have on me by the time I'm finished. And you'll notice it's not blue."

I remembered when I met her in Sunday school class with all the blue, and said, "Hey that's right, you're trying something new. What color is that?"

"Well it's got some blue in it, and some red, and I forgot what else. It's a nice shade of light purple, don't you think?" she replied.

"Yes it is. I'm sure it will be beeeauuutiiiful when you're done and get everything back together again," I said.

"That's right," she acknowledged. "Getting ready to paint and getting everything back in place is the hardest part, I think. Maybe you can help me move my furniture back when I'm done.

"You betcha, be glad to," I agreed.

It was nice to be getting better acquainted with Miss Leona. She was already beginning to feel like family. After lunch she went back to her painting and I went over home to stir whatever Mom had cooking in the slow cooker. Then I headed for my grass-cutting job.

I pushed my lawnmower in front of Mr. Charleston's house. He lived five houses down the street from us on the other side. Mr. Charleston isn't much taller than I am but probably twice as heavy. In the past I'd pictured him as a good jolly St. Nick. Like Miss Leona, he was always cheerful. He laughed a lot.

Mr. Charleston owns the grocery store a couple blocks away from his house. Mom always buys our groceries there. Now that he's getting older, he just opens and closes and his staff pretty much runs the place.

Because flowers are a big interest of his, I have to be real careful not to let grass clippings fly into his flower beds. He likes my work, and always gives me more than I ask for when it's pay time.

As I cut the grass I began to wonder about the F.A.T.C.A.T. meeting later. What mystery would we be trying to solve next? Even the cats had seemed on edge when I went in to check on them this morning. They kept jumping around and talking (meowing and mewing). I think they were asking questions. I didn't take the time to put their hats on. Figured conversation could wait until later.

When I finished cutting Mr. Charleston's yard he came running out with the newspaper that had just been delivered. He was waving it around and slapping it against his leg.

"You're in the news, Teddy," he said in an excited voice.

Opening the newspaper to the second page, he pointed to the headline, "Missing Pets Found." He quickly read it aloud.

> Detective Ross DuBoss and Junior
> Detective Teddy Tessleman have
> Solved the missing pets mystery.
> Arrested for the crime are Orval
> And Ivan Krewger.....................

It went on to mention the arrest of Benjamin "Bones" Bailey, a wanted jewel thief, earlier in the week.

I had mixed feelings about the article. It was nice to get the recognition, but I was sure there would be questions, a lot of questions. We had to be careful. We didn't want the F.A.T.C.A.T. to become public knowledge yet.

My question at this point was, would Ross now be more confident in the F.A.T.C.A.T. or would they still have to prove themselves? He had to admit that two crimes had been solved and criminals apprehended without using any police. That should mean something since there were never enough police to cover everything.

I went back to help Miss Leona. She had just finished cleaning her painting tools.

I looked at the room. "Are you ready to move everything back? It is beautiful, very nice color. I like it."

"Thank you, and thank you for coming back to help me," Miss Leona said. "I've got a fresh apple pie I made this morning before I started painting. Would you like a snack before we start work? It's only 3 o'clock."

"Oh yeah! And, thanks for telling me the time. I need to run home first to stir the slow cooker a bit. I almost forgot," I said.

After a great piece of apple pie and helping Miss Leona put her furniture back, I was off to cut the other yard I had scheduled.

"See you later, Miss Leona," I said.

When I went home, put the mower away, and went inside to get ready for dinner.

Mom was home and so was Miss Leona. The table was set. The smell of Mom's cooking filled the air. Um, um, good! Even though I had an afternoon snack, I was hungry.

It didn't seem like five hours had passed since lunch. So much was going on. In a short time Ross would be filling me in on our new case and I felt like I might explode with anticipation.

As the last bite of chicken slid down my throat I sighed with pleasure.

"Thanks Mom. Couldn't have been better. I'm sorry, can I go? I gotta see Ross." "Yes dear," said Mom, as I flew out the door.

Ross was just pulling in the driveway and when we walked into the house, we found all four cats all lined up just inside the door. They reminded me of four happy puppies that had not seen anyone for a week. Usually they would have been lying around napping, but not today. As soon as we got inside they were off, each one stopping under the peg that held their hat and one by one the hats went on while the remarks and questions spilled out.

CHAPTER SEVEN
BROKEN LOCKS

Bobbie Lee's hat went on first. Hardly had it gone on than her remarks came out. "So what's the scoop, Boss?"

As quickly as Billie Rose's hat was snapped into place, she asked, "What's going on Ross buddy?"

Then came Moon Sun, "What's happening, Boss Ross? Tell me quick. Who are we after?

Finally Big M, with his hat in place, looked around, shook his head, and calmly said, "Just give us the facts, Ross, just the facts. I'm ready to formulate a stratagem. I'm sure I can devise a scheme that will outwit the most clever villain."

Ross said, "Thank you, M&M. I will be happy to hear your plan when you are ready. Here's our new challenge."

The cats all settled down and Ross began. He told us that the new case was actually a little weird. All around Midtown, businesses and residences were reporting broken locks. Doors were unlocked, but nothing was reported missing. There were no robberies. Only the locks were broken and the doors could not be locked. In each case repairs had to be made so the buildings could be secured.

Our job was to find out who or what was breaking locks. "Where do we begin?" That was my question.

Ross answered, "That is the question, Teddy. Think about it. Now, I have two more things before we break up our meeting. Teddy, don't forget the Wednesday night Junior Detective meeting. It's special. Now I have something else special to share. I have installed a switch on the side of the cats' hats."

Ross reached down and put the switch on Bobbie Lee's hat to the "on" position.

"Talk to us, Bobbie Lee," he said.

Bobbie Lee said, "It's nice to get a new case to work on, Boss."

"Yes it is Bobbie Lee," said Ross. "Now, turn on your speaker and say, "Stop, you're under arrest."

"STOP! YOU'RE UNDER ARREST!" Her voice, which didn't sound a bit like hers came roaring out of her speaker.

"Wow, that's what I'm talking about!" I said. "That'll get their attention!" All the cats flipped the toggle switches on and began shouting commands. "HANDS UP!"

"TURN AROUND AND FACE THE WALL!" "GO AHEAD, SCUMBAG, MAKE MY DAY!"

Moon Sun flipped his switch off and said, "Heard that in that movie you were watching the other evening, Ross. Detective Callahan, he is one cool dude."

Big M roared out his comment, "THAT IS AN EXEMPLARY MODIFICATION TO THE DEVICE, IMPECCABLE. TEDDY, MARVELOUS IDEA. ROSS, INCREDIBLE JOB. AWESOME, AWESOME."

Ross flipped off his switch. I think the house was beginning to shake.

I said, "That's even better than I imagined. That will make the bad guys take notice. These little guys sound scary. I was called a tiger today at football practice. Now I gotta say you cats sound at least as ferocious as a tiger. I know the Bible says, *Gentle words turn away wrath, and harsh words stir up anger.* We can leave the kind gentle words to Ross after the C.A.T. has got the crook's attention and he makes the arrest."

Big M spoke up, "Yes Teddy, we aren't out to yell harsh words to these criminals, but when F.A.T.C.A.T. catches them in the act, we must bestow on them a racket that will resonate our usual feline tones into a reverberation that will shake the very walls around them. This will stop them in their tracks so that our fearless leader, Boss Ross, can snap the shackles on them."

"Yes, whatever you say, Big M," I responded.

Ross broke in, "Okay, team, we need to get out there and collect clues so we can begin to set up some strategies. Like Big M said, make a plan."

"Is that what he said?" I questioned.

"Yes, in a manner of speaking," responded Ross. "He does have a manner of speaking, a style, a mode of presentation. Maybe we've created a monster here in giving him the ability to communicate. He seems to have picked up a big vocabulary from his previous owner, the professor, at the university.

I knew Ross was probably thinking the same thing but I asked, "Do you think if we visited the places where locks have been broken we could uncover some clues?"

Ross replied, "Good idea, Teddy. It's getting late and we are going to lose daylight today. Let's try to get together tomorrow afternoon. We'll visit the last two sites where broken locks have been reported. Maybe we will see something that will give us a clue."

We ended our meeting. I walked out of the house to find it was night. It seemed only minutes ago that I entered the house with Ross to find four very excited cats. Now I was going home in the dark, wondering what tomorrow would bring and if I could sleep.

Morning came. Mom was gone, but she left me one of her notes to wish me a good day. "I love you, Teddy, God loves you. He will look out for you.

Remember, Miss Leona is there for you also." Yes, Mom, I thought. I didn't feel like I needed to check in with Miss Leona all the time. I knew God was always with me, but it was good that Miss Leona was there.

I was glad when it was time to investigate the last two sites where broken locks were reported. We decided to take the cats. They might notice something at their level of observation. Also, we really didn't need to go inside the buildings since the crimes happened outside the entry doors.

The first door was on an office at a construction site. It was a trailer that had been parked a little off the actual building area where most of the workers were busy. We left the cats inside the car because there were so many people and so much traffic. We didn't want them to get spooked or squished.

Ross said, "Cats, sit up at the back window and watch for anything suspicious while Teddy and I take a closer look. We'll need for you to get out and observe more closely at the next site."

"You got it, Boss," said Bobbie Lee. "Hear you talking," said Billie Rose. "Got it covered, Ross," said Moon Sun.

"As you direct, I shall execute," responded Big M.

The ground around the trailer was a little soft. The foreman told us there had been a water leak a few days back. The lock had been broken two days ago. I noticed footprints that started by some tire tracks, like someone had stepped out of a vehicle before walking up to the step going into the trailer. Strange thing was they were made with bare feet. I wondered why anyone would take off their shoes to go into a trailer on a construction site. And why walk on the soft ground first? "Why wouldn't they take off their shoes by the step?" I asked Ross.

He said, "That is peculiar, Teddy. Good observation."

The second site was somebody's house not too far from the station where we had found the missing pets. As we looked around the area just outside the door with the broken lock, Bobbie Lee sneezed. I looked down at her just as she sneezed again. Something red flew up in front of her. I picked it up. It looked like lint or fuzz from clothing. Other than this piece of red fuzz there was not a clue around. Of course Ross checked for fingerprints. The only prints were from the residents of the home. Some were smudged. "Maybe someone wore gloves to avoid leaving prints," I said.

"Yes," said Ross. "And someone might have taken off shoes to avoid leaving shoeprints."

"On a crime drama that Mom and I occasionally watch, a criminal was caught by comparing a shoe print found at the crime scene with the shoe worn by the guilty person."

"It would be much more difficult to match a barefoot print than a shoe print, especially if the foot had a sock on it," Ross added.

Later, back at Ross's house, we sat down to discuss our findings. I offered a possible theory, "What if the person doing this is removing their shoes to not leave shoe prints? What if they were wearing red socks that left some fuzz caught by the rough concrete outside that house? Not barefeet, but feet with red socks?"

"Red socks and broken locks," snickered Moon Sun. "I'm a poet and don't know it."

Big M added, "It rhymes, my friend, but I highly doubt if it will turn out to be incriminating evidence."

Ross said, "So far, so good. We'll try to investigate some more sites this week.

Maybe something will come together."

The next day after I had done my chores for the day, I went home to get ready for the monthly Junior Detective meeting. A photo album was sitting on the dining room table. Whatever Mom had cooking in the slow cooker for supper smelled very inviting, tempting me to lift the lid for a look-see. I resisted. Figured it would be time to eat soon enough.

Sitting down, I opened the book, and began turning the picture covered pages. It started with pictures of Mom and Dad before I was born. Then there were many pictures of me as I grew up through the first 12 years of my life. On the last page Mom had put a picture she"d taken of me and Big M. I was holding him outside the station where the Krewger Brothers were keeping the stolen pets, right after we rescued him. Beside the picture she had put the article from the newspaper. She had added another new page. I wondered what she was going to put on it.

I went back to a picture of Dad that was taken just before he left two years ago. He was in his dress uniform, his beret set slightly to the side. He was smiling, standing beside his duffle bag with his hand held up waving goodbye. Little did we know that instead of a couple of weeks, or months, it would be over two years. My eyes filled to overflowing, and tears ran down my face, falling on the album page. Ten months, ten whole months. Would he ever come back? I said a prayer sitting there at the dining room table, asking God for my dad to safely return soon. Matthew 19:26. A scripture I memorized says, *"With God all things are possible."*

The door opened and Mom said, "Hi Sunshine, how are you doing?"

She noticed my tear-streaked face when she came over and saw I'd been looking at Dad's picture. She wrapped her arms around me. "I miss him too, sweetheart. It's good to look at the pictures once in a while, even if it does make us sad. We'll have those good times again. Keep your chin up."

"Thanks, Mom, I know we will, but it's been so long," I said.

"Yes it has, Teddy, but Jesus gives us strength when we are at our weakest. Physical, emotional, mental and spiritual, "everything" doesn't leave anything out. Remember that."

She ruffled my hair and said, "Let's eat and get ready to go to your meeting.

Ross invited me to come with you. He said it's a special meeting."

"What's special?" I asked. "We usually just talk about what everyone has been doing and maybe watch a training video of some kind. It's not that our meetings aren't interesting and useful, but they're not what I'd call special."

"Oh well, whatever it is, I'd like to go if you don't mind," Mom said as she filled two bowls with the stew from the slow cooker.

It seems like only yesterday that Ross started the "Youth to Law Enforcement Affirmation Program." Youth LEAP for short. We leap into this program ready to discover and confirm that law enforcement is the direction we want to go in our careers. That's what Ross told us. He only wanted kids to join if they were seriously interested in finding out more about law enforcement.

I am a Junior Detective Level One, JDL1. You have to have a sponsor and you have to be twelve to sixteen years old. We start at JDL1 and advance to JDL2 and JDL3 if we satisfy the requirements. Then, if we stick with it, we can become Junior Detective Third Class. Promotions continue until we reach JD First Class, JD1C.There is a big ceremony like you are graduating from college or something. That's my goal.

They say if a kid stays in the program that long they are destined for law enforcement. Right now, I know I want to be a special-forces soldier like my dad, or a detective like Ross. Either way I know my dad would be proud. Make the world a safer place. That's what they do. That's what I want to do.

About an hour later we walked into Ross's Sunday school room were five other Junior Detectives, Ross, and the five other mentors were waiting. A banner was stretched across the front of the room.

"You knew all about this, didn't you?" I said to Mom.

She smiled a mischievous smile and shrugged her shoulders.

CHAPTER EIGHT
RED SOCKS AND BROKEN LOCKS

The banner said in big bold letters.

GOOD JOB, TEDDY!

Junior Detective Second Level

Now I knew what the new page in the photo album was for. Mom knew I was going to get the promotion. The Chief of Police of the Midtown Police Department gave a little speech about entering into law enforcement. Then Ross was ready to make the presentation.

"Teddy, please come up and receive your award," announced Ross.

"For your contribution in the apprehension of Bones Bailey, Orval and Ivan Krewger, and mastering the educational requirements for the second level of the Junior Detective program, I am honored to present to you this certificate of achievement and your first tassel. Congratulations!"

Wow! After just seven months, helping Ross with a couple of cases, some trial runs with the cats or, I should say, F.A.T.C.A.T. Now this! I was one step closer to my goal. YES!

I was certain at this point that I wanted to follow in my dad's footsteps or be like Ross. My mom was proud of me. My dad would have been also. I was pretty pleased with myself too.

Six hats flew into the air. Mine first followed by the other five cadets. They congratulated me and patted me on the back saying, "Great job, Teddy." But they did not know the underlying ingredient to our success, the F.A.T.C.A.T.

A bright red tassel would now hang from my hat if I could find it. As I went to retrieve it, someone slapped me on the back and said, "Hey Tiger, this is a big deal, huh? I'm here to meet my granddad."

I looked around and of all people, it was Sam.

"My granddad is going to dinner with me and my mom. We were supposed to meet him here after this meeting. I peeked in the door and saw what was going on. Had to come in. So I guess this is pretty neat stuff," said Sam.

"Your granddad? I enquired. "Yeah, Chief Edding."

I don't know why I didn't think of a possible connection before. Guess I was so used to hearing him called Chief, that the Edding part never crossed my mind.

"Granddad asked me to check out the JD program. Looks like Boy Scouts to me." Sam jested.

"Well, Sam, I'm sure you would enjoy the program," I encouraged him. "Maybe we can talk about it someday before or after football practice. I'd be glad to tell you what I know. I guess I'm pretty up on everything. Hey, before you go, let me introduce you to my mom and Ross DuBoss, my mentor."

We walked to the table where my mom and Ross were sitting

"Mom and Ross, look who I found. Or, I guess he found me. This is Sam Edding, the Chief's grandson. We are football teammates. Sam gets everyone out of the way so I can run the ball. He wants to find out more about the JD program."

Ross reached across the table to shake hands, "Hi Sam, the chief told me he was trying to encourage his grandson to join the program. I understand Detective Iverson is looking for a cadet to mentor. Maybe we can match up you two if you decide to apply."

"Thank you. That would be great. I'll give it some thought. Well, I think I better go find Granddad. It's nice to meet you both. Catch you tomorrow at practice, Teddy," said Sam as he went to join the chief who was sitting across the room.

I couldn't believe this was the guy who'd tried to flatten me on the first day of summer practice. He still came off a bit sarcastic and smart-alecky, but he was showing a possible interest in the JD program. It could be a way for me to get to know what makes this guy tick. I just hoped it wasn't a big act.

The evening was winding down. The other cadets and their mentors came by to congratulate me again on their way out. Mom and I were ready to head out also. It had been a great evening, full of surprises.

On the way home I told Mom about how Sam had seemed to want to destroy me the first few days of football practice.

Mom said, "Well dear, I can tell you some things that might help you understand his behavior. Sam lost his dad a few months ago. He has struggled with his loss. I'm sure you can understand that. Coincidentally, his mom works with me at the real estate agency.

She told me she had a very difficult time with Sam for a while. His anger still flares up once in a while. But, he is getting better. He is learning how to accept his loss and go on with his life. He has accepted counseling from Pastor Bill at our church."

I guess Sam and I had more in common than I realized. This was another connection I might use to get along with this guy.

It wasn't too late when we got home so I went out on the deck to see what the critters were up to. My mind was full. I didn't know if I wanted to think about all the stuff I had discovered or just let it all go and enjoy the squirrels for a little while. The squirrels won. It was no contest when they started doing their thing. They chased each other, chattered and looked straight at me as though to say, "Hey, this entertainment is not for free, how about filling up the feeders?"

After I hit the sack, my thoughts turned to the last few weeks. We'd had two quick successes with the C.A.T. But this new case was different. Nothing was being taken.

Things were being broken. Ross had not been able to gather any helpful information or good leads. We investigated the other sites, but saw nothing. Broken lock, no fingerprints, no footprints, at least none from shoes.

At the last site we visited the repair guy was just arriving as we were leaving. He drove a yellow van that had red lettering on the side that said,

MAX LEE'S SECURITY SYSTEMS

Installation and Repair
Locksmith
MAXIMUM SERVICE
LEE HAS THE KEY

I suggested to Ross, "Maybe we could talk to the repair people that are working on the broken locks."

Ross nodded, "Couldn't hurt. I'll find out whose making repairs."

Ross caught me early the next morning when I was at his house with the cats.

"Would you believe there are only two locksmiths in Midtown? Only one of them repairs broken locks. In each case the damage is such that the locks must be replaced. Max Lee is taking care of all of them. I checked his repair schedule. Can you be available this afternoon around two o'clock? He's working on a lock at a residence that we haven't looked at."

"Can we take the cats?" I asked. "They haven't been out for a while I think they're getting cabin fever."

"I believe you're right," Ross agreed. "We've been on this case for three weeks. We have to make something happen."

"I could take the cats on my bike if it's not too far! We can let them kind of hide out and see what they see," I suggested.

Ross agreed and left for work. I decided to have a chat with the cats to let them know that they would be going out later. I put their hats on and described our plan for the afternoon.

"Good deal," said Bobbie Lee.

Billie Rose spoke up, "Yes, Teddy, we are getting cabin fever. We haven't been out in forever."

Moon Sun came on, "I thought maybe we had been laid off, or maybe being replaced with parrots."

"Ha, ha, ha! Fat chance, Moon, surely you jest. My colleagues are realizing the gravity of the situation and the significance of our contribution and assistance. Am I right, Teddy, my boy?" said Big M.

"Yes, Big M, of course we need you," I said, laughing not because of what he said, but because it is so funny to see a cat laugh.

I took off the cat's hats and hung them up, and left for football practice. I got there a little early.

Sam was already there. He greeted me and asked, "Want to talk about the JD program a little before we get ready for practice? We have about twenty minutes before we need to go to the locker room."

Sam seemed more serious than usual. He looked me square in the eyes and said, "Teddy, I want to try to explain something to you. I need to tell you I'm sorry for the way I treated you when we first started football practice. I was just upset and angry. When I put the gear on, it kind of made me feel powerful and mean and then I saw you. It could have been anyone, but it was you. I headed for you. I wanted to run over you, try my shoulder pads out on you. You're pretty quick. You ducked me and I lost my balance and landed face first in the dirt. That made me even angrier. If the coach hadn't called us to the practice field, I probably would have been all over you for no reason. It was stupid."

I said, "I think I know why you were in a bad mood."

"Let me explain," Sam said. "I lost my dad a while back. I can't keep my mind off it. I get angry because he isn't here. I'm only trying out for football because he and I always enjoyed it so much. I haven't wanted to do much of anything. Dad always liked to pass the football around with me. So, I decided that maybe playing football would make me feel closer to him. When I got here, I felt so alone. It made me mad."

"Been there, done that." I said. "I've lost my dad too. At least he's been gone for over ten months now. I know my dad is only missing so I can't relate entirely to what you're going through. But I miss him a lot."

"Me too," said Sam. "Mom talked me into counseling sessions with Pastor Bill at the church. He's been able to help me see things better and kind of understand."

"I hear you talkin," I agreed. "I've got Mom, and I lean on Ross a lot. It's not easy to keep your chin up and keep on keeping on. I'm not ashamed to say I breakdown from time to time."

Sam looked at the ground and kicked the dust. "Yeah, I try not to, tell myself I gotta be tough. Guess that's why I really get mad. I can't let it go, you know. We haven't talked much about the JD program, have we? Now that we have buried the hatchet, so to speak, maybe we can lean on each other sometime when we need to."

Other guys were coming in for practice. As we started for the locker room, I grabbed Sam's arm. "We'll talk later, right? We can be here for each other, right!"

Sam looked at me and smiled. "Again, I'm sorry Teddy. Please forgive me?" "No problem," I said. "Let's go play football."

Later, at around 1:00 p.m. I went to get the cats. Ross had left me a note and what looked like a cell phone ear bud. It wrapped around the ear and laid against the side of the face. Anyone seeing it would think it was for a cell phone. But why did he leave it?

I read the note.

Meet me at 627 Locust Ave. Back door. Keep the cats in the shrubbery so they won't be noticed. Just put their collars on. I think that would be best this time. I've made receivers that will make it possible for us to communicate with them when they are

> **wearing their collars. We won't have the advantage of their speakers or BIG voices. We shouldn't need them this time. Nobody will suspect that we are communicating with them. This might be a good time to give it a try.**

This seemed like a good idea. I put their collars on and did a little test. With my ear bud in place I said, "Do you hear me?"

Nothing.

Bobbie Lee jumped up on the table and pointed to the note with her paw. Then I saw the **P.S.**

> **Almost forgot. You will find a wire on the top edge of their collars with a small bead-shaped object on it. Raise it so it is by their ears. They will be able to hear you then.**

I did that, "Do you hear me?" I said.

Bobbie Lee said, "Yes, Teddy. Do you hear me?"

"Great, I guess we're in business. Let's load up and hit the road." "Big M spoke up, "Please have mercy, not the tandem taxi again!"

"Come on, M&M, you know you love it," I teased. "You can stay here if you want." "You know better than that, Teddy. I don't mean to be rude, but I'm just afraid that another ride on that velocipede machine of yours might be detrimental to my wellbeing," he said.

I assured M&M, "I'll be extra careful. I won't hit any big bumps or huge holes, and I'll keep my whatever you said machine in an upright position. Can we go now?"

We arrived at the house where the lock repair man was going to be working. I told the F.A.T.C.A.T. to find a place to blend into the landscape.

Ross pulled into the driveway right behind Max Lee's big yellow van. They exchanged pleasantries and Mr. Lee told his assistant, a tall lanky young man, to get his toolbox and a new lock. He headed for the back door. He was looking at the lock as though trying to decide what to do next.

I felt something poking me in my ankle. I looked down to see Moon Sun pointing with his paw to something obvious from his point of view.

He whispered, "Check out the socks."

CHAPTER NINE
LOCK BUMPING

Back to the bushes Moon Sun headed, as Max Lee, who obviously liked red, said, "What a cute kitty."

"Grrrrrrr," I heard Moon Sun say.

I was glad Moon Sun wasn't wearing his hat. He might have given Mr. Lee a big voice, "GRRRRRR."

Mr. Lee wore a red baseball hat and a red tee shirt with the words *Max Lee's Security Systems, Lee has the key* across the back. And lastly, barely visible under his blue jean pant legs, were fuzzy red socks.

Ross remarked, "I heard you tell your assistant to bring a new lock. How did you know you would need to replace it?"

Max Lee shrugged his shoulders, "They've all needed to be replaced so far. Just figured this one would probably be the same. I've ordered more locks."

"Why couldn't they be repaired?" I asked.

"Keys are broken off in them. Something has been injected into the lock, then a key inserted and broken off. Whatever is injected into the lock makes it impossible to remove the key. New lock, it's the only way," Max said.

"Is there anything the locks have in common other than that?" I asked.

Max Lee pointed at the lock, "They've all had pin and tumbler locking mechanisms. I install Smart Key locks. They have a side-locking bar technology, which is an improvement to the traditional pin and tumbler design. It prevents lock bumping, a technique where an intruder with a specially cut key can 'bump' a lock open using skilled strikes to the key in the lock. All the locks have been bumped to open the doors, then jammed and plugged with a broken key."

"How many more have you been called to fix?" I asked. "None for now," he answered.

The thought occurred to me that if that were the case, why had Mr. Lee ordered more locks? Could it be, was it possible? Surely not. Max Lee couldn't be drumming up business for himself by going around breaking locks so he would be called to fix them, would he?

Max yelled at his assistant, "Where's that lock? Get a move on. We don't have all day."

Something about this man just seemed strange. Obviously Moon Sun had taken a dislike for him. I could hear his low throaty growl from off behind one of the evergreen shrubs along the walk. I couldn't see him, but I knew he wasn't far away.

Bait! I thought. Maybe we should dangle some bait in front of this Max Lee fish. I walked over to where Ross was finishing some of the paper work he always had to do when he made an investigative stop.

"Ross, can I speak with you over by your car for a sec?" "Sure, Teddy. What's up?"

"Does anything strike you as suspicious about this character?" I asked.

"Well, I have found some peculiar problems with him and this case. Why do you ask?" inquired Ross.

"Remember how well the bait worked in our last case?" I asked. "Yes. And?" questioned Ross.

"Do you mind if I dangle a little something in front of Max Lee?" I continued. Ross grinned at me. "Do it, Teddy. I trust your instincts."

I walked back to where Max Lee was working, and tried to engage him in some small talk."Mr. Lee, did you do the security system on the Charleston Grocery Store.

"Yes, as a matter of fact, I did," Max answered.

I mentioned, "The last time I cut Mr. Charleston's grass he told me they were going to do some work on the store. They were going to be closed next Monday and Tuesday evening." With that I considered the bait placed.

Max Lee finished the lock. He gave the homeowner the keys, and headed for his van. "Max shouted at his assistant, "Grab that box and those tools. Hurry up."

Ross chatted with him for a bit and I went to the alley where I had left my bike behind a storage shed.

"Let's go, C.A.T.," I said into my mic.

Four cats flew out of the bushes and jumped up into the basket for a surprisingly quiet ride home. Once back at Ross's house they were ready to talk and formulate a plan, as Big M. put it.

Moon Sun was repeating over and over, "Red socks and broken locks, red socks and broken locks, Teddy, he had red socks."

Bobbie Lee offered, "You do remember the red fuzz we found at one of the sites, don't you?"

Billie Rose said, "And he does take off his shoes when he is breaking the locks."

M&M added, "Look, my fellow felines; a piece of red fuzz and the red socks worn by this Lee character is not conclusive anything. We need more!" added M&M.

"Right you are, M&M. We need more. And I think Teddy may have it," said Ross.

I began to explain my idea, "I told Max Lee that the Charleston Grocery Store would be closed next Monday and Tuesday evening because they are remodeling. This would be a perfect opportunity for him to slip back behind the store and do his thing if he is the one breaking locks. We can hide behind the trash dumpster or in the area where he flattens cardboard boxes and stacks them for recycling."

"Yes, and if he goes for it, we nab him," said Moon Sun.

"Alright, I think we've got ourselves a plan. We'll have a nice relaxing weekend and maybe Monday we'll get lucky," said Ross.

I had to get home. Mom had planned on taking me and Miss Leona out to dinner to a new restaurant she wanted to try.

As I walked into the house, Mom said, "Oh good, Teddy, you're home. I've asked Lois Edding and Sam to join us. They are to meet us here at 6:00 You have an hour to get ready."

"Great!" I responded. "I want to get better acquainted with Sam.. Cool, Mom, good deal."

It would be nice to spend time with Sam and his mom. We all seemed to have a lot in common. I also welcomed the chance to visit with Sam away from football practice.

Football practice was good time, but we were both always very focused on the game. I walked into the kitchen just as Mom began to call me, and then the doorbell rang.

Sam and his mom were there.

"Hi, Lois, hi, Sam," Mom said. "Come in for a minute. We're about ready."

Sam's eyes found the pictures on the mantle and the crossed swords on the wall above the gas fireplace.

"What are the swords for?" he asked. "Are they just decoration, or do they mean something?"

I walked to the mantle and put my hands on one of the swords.

"Well, the picture below the swords is my dad's dad. He died in combat. The downward-pointing swords mean that the fight is over. It's a memorial to those who fought and died in battle. It also means what it says on the plaque beside the picture."

I read, "No more killing, no more battles, and no more wars. It is then that mankind will have finally realized that the only thing that can fight and conquer evil is love. Jesus said, love is not violent."

"Cool," said Sam. "I hate violence, believe it or not."

I said in a breaking voice, "My dad followed in his dad's footsteps. I'm very proud of them both. My granddad is gone. My dad is missing, as you know."

I saw Mom pick up her purse and was glad. I sometimes get a little emotional when I talk of my granddad and missing dad.

I could tell Mom was eager to leave too. "We'd better go. The restaurant might be crowded."

We all got in Mom's car and started the four-block trip to the Active Life Buffet and Grill. As we passed Charleston's Grocery Store I noticed Lee's familiar yellow van in the parking lot. I wondered where the driver might be. Was he grocery shopping, or like us, checking out the new restaurant next door? Then I noticed he was sitting behind the steering wheel. Could he be scoping out a possible new crime caper? I asked myself. Of course, I was guessing, that he was the villain.

Inside the restaurant we were quickly seated. I was hungry. Sam and I were fascinated by the decorations. The restaurant was called the Active Life Buffet and Grill.

Sam spoke up, "Wow! Look at all this stuff."

The walls were plastered with all kinds of sporting paraphernalia. There's another word that I probably learned from Big M. Pictures of athletes in action were everywhere amongst the baseball bats, tennis rackets, ball gloves, hockey sticks, golf clubs, you name it. If it had anything to do with sports, you could probably find it somewhere.

"I don't know if I want to eat or just check out all the decorations," Sam said.

Once we were seated and had been given our plates, we could go fill them with whatever we wanted from the many foods ready for us to choose from. My plate wasn't big enough to hold everything I wanted to try but, I could go back for seconds, which was a good thing. Then for dessert there were cakes, pies, cookies, puddings, jello, ice cream, whoa! This place was amazing. Sam and I both had healthy appetites. I'm sure we got our mom's money's worth. Our moms and Miss Leona ate like moms concerned about their weight, all the while commenting about how good everything was.

Mom said, "This vegetable frittata is wonderful."

Sam's mom said, "Oh this shrimp primavera is delicious." Miss Leona said, "And the crab soufflé is amazing."

Sam and I said, "Yeah, it's great." and went back for seconds.

We ate, we talked, we laughed, and we had a real good time. An hour passed so fast I couldn't believe it. Leaving I noticed the yellow van was gone. I hoped he had accomplished what he came for, and that making a plan to create the need for another lock replacement was his objective.

When we got to our house, Sam and I made plans to meet Saturday afternoon to throw the football around for a little while. I needed to practice catching, and Sam needed a friend.

Mom woke me up the next morning. "Rise and shine, Sunshine," she said with the big smile she always woke me up with.

The sun was already shining in my bedroom window. I hoped Mom and I would shine for Miss Leona at our piano lesson. We had been practicing a duet and wanted to play it for her.

After all the food I had eaten the evening before, I didn't want much breakfast. Mom had set out the cereal and some orange juice. I took it out on the deck where she was watching the birds. The little squirrels were chattering in the trees. One of them came down and took a spot in the platform feeder, picked up a peanut, sat back and began to nibble while keeping an eye on us.

Mom and I smiled as it finished one nut and started another. "I'm surprised it's sitting there eating with us so close," I said.

"Yes, maybe they're realizing we won't bother them," Mom replied. It was relaxing watching the squirrel eat while I ate too.

We left the squirrel to his peanuts, got our music, and headed for Miss Leona's.

She met us at the door, patted her stomach and said, "Mercy, I should not have eaten so much last night."

I laughed. "You guys eat like birds. Now, Sam and me, we put it away."

"Well, you're growing, active boys," said Miss Leona. "You need to fuel the furnace.

It was good though, wasn't it?" "Yes it was," I agreed.

Mom said, "We'd like for you to critique a duet we have been working on. It's one of Teddy's dad's favorites. We want to play it for him when he comes home."

"Wonderful! So glad you're working on something together," said Miss Leona.

After Mom and I played our piece for her, she helped us smooth out some rough edges. Then Mom started going over her lesson. We had improved a lot during these few weeks of lessons.

I sat in a chair by the window. My thoughts wandered as Mom played. It's amazing how things change when you work at it. Our piano-playing, the little squirrel's trust, the cases we work on, the cats, the equipment we've developed and use with them, football, me and Sam's friendship, and the list goes on. God causes everything to come together for good. I read that in Romans 8:28. It was a memory verse, and it's true. I know the world changes around us, but God is changeless and dependable. Look at Sam and how he's changed.

"Okay, Teddy," said Miss Leona.

Mom had finished her lesson and it was my turn. After I played my lesson, Mom had shopping to do and I was going to cut some grass. I was glad the grass growing was slowing down a bit. School would start soon and with football practice and working with Ross and the C.A.T., my grass cutting time was going to be limited.

I pushed my mower over to Mr. Charleston's. The grass wasn't in bad shape but Mr. Charleston wanted me to cut it every week even when it wasn't growing much. I was glad, because I wanted to talk to him about the stakeout that Ross and I had tentatively planned for Monday evening and if needed, Tuesday.

I was careful not to send clippings into the flowerbeds. When I finished and swept the grass off his walk, I rang the doorbell.

"Hi, Teddy," said Mr. Charleston as he opened the door and handed me my money. "Do you have a minute, Mr. Charleston?

"Certainly, Teddy, what's on your mind?"

I asked, "Have you heard about all the lock-breaking going on here in Midtown?" "Yes, and I keep hoping it won't happen to me. So far I've had no problems." "That's what I want to talk to you about," I said.

I explained how Ross and I planned to watch his store Monday and Tuesday evenings when he would be closed, just in case the lock-breaker had any idea about bumping his locks.

"What do you mean, bumping?" he asked.

I went on to explain bumping as Mr. Lee had described it to Ross and me. "Do I need to be there?"

"No, it would be best if you're not," I told him.

He thanked me and said, "I hope whoever is doing this will be caught in the act." "Me too," I assured him.

The plan was now in place. I'd finalize everything with Ross tomorrow.

I got home just in time to help Mom unload the groceries from her car trunk. She had one of the biggest watermelons I had ever seen.

"If you'd like we can have a slice with our lunch," Mom said.

"Yes!" Watermelon is a big favorite at our house.

That afternoon I headed for the football practice field, and saw Sam standing at the top of the bleachers. I rode over and parked my bike. Sam threw the ball in my direction.

"Be alive, Tiger, be alive," he called out.

I caught the ball and ran up the steps to join him.

"Do you realize that school starts in two weeks, Teddy?"

"Yeah, I was thinking about that this morning."

"And, on Friday of our first week we play the Zephyr Zebras."

"Zephyr Zebras, where do you reckon they got a name like that?" I asked. "Must have been named after someone, I guess," he suggested.

"Do you think the Midtown Wizards might need a little magic to beat 'em?"

"Naaaa, I hear Midtown has one of the best running backs around, and one of the best guards to keep the opponents off him," Sam said laughing.

"I'm gonna remember you said that the first time I get smeared, man."

"Ahhhh, you're gonna do great. We both are. Let's throw the ball around. Go out for a long one."

Sam threw the ball with just the right amount of lead. I caught it continuing to run. We practiced until we were both breathing hard.

As we headed over to the bleachers for a break, I said, "You got a good arm, Sam, and you're accurate. Does the coach know how good you can throw?"

"Don't know. Doesn't matter, Danny's a good quarterback. Besides I like being a guard. Someone has to protect the backs so we can score points and win games. Right?"

"Yeah, I, right, and if anyone can do it, you can," I agreed.

We saw someone walking on the track toward us. It was the coach.

He said, "Just happened to see you boys throwing the ball around as I was driving by, so I stopped to watch. Been sitting over there in my car. You've got an amazing arm there,

Sam. Hadn't noticed that before. How about being my backup quarterback?"

"Thanks, Coach, but I really like playing guard," Sam answered.

"Consider it, Sam. We might need you someday. I know you know the plays from a guard's point of view. Maybe you could broaden that viewpoint as we go along."

"Sure, Coach. I pretty much already know what everyone is supposed to do. But I'll pay attention. I love the game, Coach."

"I know you do, Sam. We're lucky to have you, lucky to have you both." He waved and walked away toward his car.

"Never know who's watching, do you?" I said.

"Nope, it's a small world. Hey, how about we call it a day, Teddy? Told my mom I'd be home around four. Better head out."

"Me too. It's been fun. Good practice. See you Monday," I said.

Sam had changed. I thought he'd be excited about the coach's comments. I couldn't help but think the attention bothered Sam a little.

Sam's kind of like the broken locks in my latest crime caper. Now he needs to be fixed. I guess that's where Pastor Bill comes in. Maybe I can help.

I started to leave, but sat down on the bottom bleacher instead. Sam changed after Coach praised him and invited him to be backup quarterback. Why? I looked to see Sam walking away. He wasn't walking in the direction of his home.

CHAPTER TEN

LEE FISH

When I rode into the driveway Ross was home, but Mom was not. So, I decided to visit the cats and maybe talk to Ross a little more about the bait trap.

Ross saw me walk up on the porch. "Come in, Teddy. Get a load of this!" He sounded as excited as a kid with a new toy.

"What's happening, Ross?"

"C.A.T., Big voice!" he commanded.

Click, click, click, click, I heard in unison and big voice control switches were on. "HANDS UP, STAY WHERE YOU ARE, DON'T MOVE!"

Click, click, click, click, again and the F.A.T.C.A.T. was ready to communicate with Ross and me.

"Hey, that's pretty cool. They've got it down. Way to go, team!" I said as I slipped on my head set and mic.

"Yes, we've been practicing. These felines are getting smarter all the time. It didn't take any time at all and they've got it down perfect," bragged Ross.

It was amazing how quickly they'd caught on to anything, even Big M, who always liked to play the ho-hum, nothing-moves-me type. But put him in a situation like our last job and his true colors come out.

"What do you think about the plan for Monday evening, Ross? Anything new we need to discuss since we're all suited up here and excited about flipping switches and talking big?"

"Hey, don't talk this down, Teddy. Remember Big Voice was your idea," Moon Sun reminded me.

"I know, Moon Sun. I'm sorry. As far as I can see, C.A.T., you're perfect. I just meant, let's keep the **momentum** rolling. Hey, M&M, how about that?"

"Yo, Teddy, now you're talking," said M&M.

Ross broke in, "I think we're set, Teddy. Very straightforward plan. I'll park my car in the parking lot in front of the store. We'll hide in back behind the dumpster. If or when someone shows up to break the lock, the F.A.T.C.A.T. will move in behind them. As soon as the door is opened, the cats will click on the Big Voice and scare the tar out of them. I'll arrest them, him, her, whatever the case may be, and it's pizza time."

"Sounds fine." "Sounds good."

"Don't forget the anchovies."

"Really, Moon Sun, my friend, keep your mind on business."

"And make those nice fat anchovies, please," noted a quartet of agreeable voices.

"I think it'll work. I think the lock bumping and lock breaking is about to stop," I said. "Okay team, we're set," said Ross.

Then we heard Click, click, click, click, and big voices blared out, "F-A-T-C-A-T, FATCAT, FATCAT, FATCAT."

"Do we have the spirit or what?" said all four cats, rolling on the floor and snickering. I'd always heard that cats had minds of their own and did things on their own terms in their own time. This is true, but these four felines, well, you know they'll be there when it counts. It's just like a good football team. Everyone does their part and it just works out.

I heard Mom drive in, so I told Ross and the cats good-bye. We saw the answering machine blinking when we entered the living room. *This is Lois Edding it said. I'm worried about Sam. Is Teddy home? Does he know where Sam might be? I'm sorry, but he's usually so prompt. If he says he'll be home at 4, he's home at 4. It's now 5 and I haven't heard from him. Please let me know if you have any information.*

Mom asked, "Do you know where Sam is?"

I told her, "I last saw him when we left the football field a little before 4. The coach surprised us with a visit. He was impressed with Sam's ability to throw the ball and offered him the backup quarterback position. Sam seemed a little bit bothered about the offer."

Mom called Lois and told her what I said.

She said, "That's a help, I think I might know where he has gone." Mom asked, "Can we help?

"It might be good if you could pick me up. This is a time when we both could use a friend."

When we arrived, Lois said, "I believe I know where he is. You said the coach praised him for doing a good job, and offered him the opportunity to be quarterback."

I said, "Yes, Coach was impressed with Sam's throwing ability."

Lois said, "Sam probably wanted to talk to his dad. I'm betting he's at Rolling Hills Cemetery. That's where his dad is."

We drove the four miles to Rolling Hills. Lois told us how to find the gravesite. There sitting on the ground by his dad's grave marker, was Sam. When he saw us, he got up and said, "I'm sorry, Mom, but I had to talk to Dad, I knew he would be happy to know that I was doing okay."

"Oh Honey, he knows, he knows," said Lois.

She embraced her son and we headed for the car. Sam put his hand on my shoulder and said, "It's cool man, no problems." I knew exactly what he meant. He had to be as close to his dad as he could be.

We dropped Sam and his mom off and went home. Sam had added some drama to our usually restful and relaxing weekend. But it was over and I could hardly wait until Monday..

At Monday's practice Sam accepted Coaches offer to be backup quarterback. My work for the day was cutting Miss Leona's yard. She was working in her garden and kept wandering around looking like she had lost something or was trying to make a decision. I didn't ask. I figured she'd tell me if she wanted. After dinner I found myself at Ross's house, ready to load up the cats for the evening's excitement.

I rode my bike with a basket full of the F.A.T.C.A.T. so if we were lucky enough to apprehend someone, Ross could take care of the suspect and we would return to base camp.

Arriving at Charleston's Grocery Store, we made ourselves as comfortable as possible. How comfortable can you be hiding behind a big blue trash dumpster and sitting on fruit crates. Ross came around from the front of the building to join us.

"Felines, are you ready to catch a lock bumper?" he asked Bobbie, Billie, Moon, and Big M.

"Yes Boss, we're ready to bust a lock bumper big time with a big voice," answered Moon Sun while the others nodded their heads, and walked back and forth swishing their tails restlessly.

It was barely dark. An owl hooted from the small wooded area behind the strip mall of which the grocery store and restaurant were a part. I'm sure that around front it was business as usual, but most of the other stores were closed by now.

The minutes turned into hours. It was 10 o'clock. The restaurant closed for the day.

All was quiet. It was perfect for the perpetrator to make his move.

Nothing, no one, 11 o'clock, nothing. Had we guessed wrong? Was Lee not our culprit? Twelve o'clock came and went. We had hoped that by now the caper would have happened.

At 2 o'clock the cats were curled up asleep. One was on my lap, one was in the basket on my bike, and two were lying under the edge of the dumpster.

Ross said, "Well, team, I think our prospective bust is not going to happen tonight.

Let's wrap it up and head out."

By three o'clock I lay on my bed unable to sleep. Listening to the night sounds outside my window, I couldn't help but wonder if the lock breaker was making an early morning visit to the grocery store.

I guess I finally dozed off because I woke to the sounds of early morning traffic on our street and the smell of freshly made coffee.

I found Mom at the kitchen table laboring over the paperwork of her latest real estate deals.

"Good morning, sweetheart," she cheerfully greeted me. "I didn't want to wake you this morning. I know you got home late or maybe I should say early-this-morning.

Judging by your lack of excitement, I presume you had no luck."

"Right you are. It was a no-show unless he turned up after we left. Ross will check it out. I'd just about bet he went back and kept watch by himself. He probably didn't want to keep me out all night. If nothing has happened, we'll give it another try tonight."

"I'd love to go watch with you, but I have a late showing tonight. Good luck. By the way, if you're up to it, Miss Leona would like your help this afternoon after lunch."

"Sure, I can do that."

The time dragged by. I had a hard time concentrating at football practice. I didn't do well. The coach asked me if I was okay.

Sam even said, "Hey, man, we won't beat the Zebras if you play like that."

"I know, I'm just really disappointed in the way a stakeout went last night. I can't get my mind off it," I said.

"It'll work out," he assured me.

"I hope so. I thought we had it all figured out. I can't talk about it right now. But I'll play better tomorrow."

"You're mighty hush-hush about your work with Ross," Sam said.

"I know, sorry. I'll clue you in some day, but for now I gotta stay quiet about it," I explained.

"That's cool, whenever you're ready. By the way, I talked to Grandpa about the JD program yesterday. I think I'll give it a try. I'm to talk to Detective Iverson sometime this week. Grandpa is going to set it up," Sam said.

"That's great! I'm sure you'll enjoy it."

I left the school and headed for Miss Leona's. I figured she was doing some more painting and needed help moving furniture. When I got there, she was sitting on the porch reading. When she set the book down I noticed the word "fish" on the cover. And, in the yard between the garage and the house, I noticed what looked like a big black plastic tub.

"Hi Teddy, are you ready for lunch?" Miss Leona asked.

"Sure am. Didn't eat much this morning. Got up late," I answered. "I hope you're not too tired. I've got a hard job for you."

"I'm never too tired to help you out, Miss Leona."

Lunch including a wonderful piece of coconut pie, which I instantly decided was another favorite food.

"Now," Miss Leona said, "I want you to dig a hole."

"Hole?" I questioned.

"Yes, please."

"Well, okay," I agreed. "What's gonna be buried?"

"A garden pond shell. I've been reading this book about raising Koi fish. I don't want to raise them, but I would like to have a couple in a small pond in my garden. They are such beautiful fish. I'll have a small fountain, and decorate it all up. I'll start small, and if they grow too big I'll let you dig a bigger hole."

"Whatever you want," I said. "It'll be good exercise."

Miss Leona helped me lay out the dimensions on the ground and I began. The ground wasn't hard, and in no time I had it dug and we set the shell in place. We worked the dirt in around it and Miss Leona was soon in the Koi business.

"The man at the store where I'm buying the fish said he would set up the pump and filters and get it all running for me when I got the shell ready. Then I'll put some plants and rocks around it," said Miss Leona.

When we finished it was late afternoon and I hadn't checked on the cats today. I knew Ross would be sure they had everything they needed before he left for work. I was just used to spending a little time with them every morning and wanted to see them.

Mom rolled in as I crossed the driveway.

"Be right back," I called out as I headed for Ross's house.

Inside the house I found Big M sitting on his stool and looking at a book. I took a look. It was about fish too. He was licking his chops. Made me wonder if I should be concerned about Miss Leona's fish. He was so into it, he hardly acknowledged my presence. Moon Sun and the girls were watching a movie. It was about a fish named Elmo. Ross taught them how to turn the TV on and change channels. He had even invented a gadget that, when attached to the TV sound, translates it so they understand what is being said. The man is a genius and he works as a detective. Go figure!

The cats were all okay and occupied, so I left them to go home and spend some time with Mom.

Mom was rattling pots and pans. "What's going on?" I asked.

"I'm going to make you guys something yummy. If you're not successful this evening and don't have a pizza celebration party, you can at least enjoy a piece of fresh apple pie. I'll fix tuna cakes for the cats," said Mom.

"You're too much, but let's hope we'll have to save it for another time. On second thought, we could have your pie and tuna cakes instead of pizza for a change," I said.

I helped Mom for a while, keeping an eye on the clock. In less than an hour we needed to be on location. The kitchen was filling with the smell of fresh baking and tuna fish cakes. I was sure we'd enjoy them after our stakeout – hopefully in celebration. Time was flying and I needed to go prepare the cats.

Big M was now sitting in front of the TV, meowing at the other cats and they were meowing back. I'm sure the conversation would have been entertaining had I been set up to understand.

I was guessing we had about a half hour before the sun would set. We needed to be in place by then. The cats must have sensed that it was time. They all went to their room and stood under the hooks holding their gear. I slipped on my headphones and mic first. Then, on went Bobbie Lee's bonnet.

"I have a good feeling about tonight, Teddy," she said.

Billie Rose's bonnet slipped over her head. "Yes, Teddy, I feel tonight's the night." she added.

Moon Sun was next. "That Lee fish will bite tonight, Teddy."

Big M came on as quickly as his helmet did. "I desire to get my teeth into the Lee fish, Teddy. We are carnivorous, you know."

I said, "I hope it's him, and he shows. But please don't go after him. Let Ross take care of that. Just click on your big voices when the time comes, and scare the daylights out of him."

With a basket full of C.A.T., I went toward Charleston's Grocery Store and I pedaled into the paved lot behind the store.

Parking behind the big blue dumpster, I heard a fluttering noise in the trees at the edge of the woods. The owl from the night before must have been spooked. He took off and flew deeper into the increasing darkness. The moon was just beginning to show through the trees. The sun on the other side of the store was out of sight. Only a red sky remained. I knew people further west were still enjoying the sunshine, but it was done with us for the day.

Ross wasn't there yet. My cell phone rang. "Teddy here," I answered.

"I'm just getting away from the office, Teddy. Sit tight. If anything should happen before I get there, do not confront! I repeat, do not confront, observe only!" cautioned Ross.

"Got it, Boss. Observe, but don't confront." Ross said, "I'm about ten minutes away." "Okay, I'll tell the F.A.T.C.A.T."

I passed the information on to the cats.

Moon Sun said, "He better get here, or M and I might get us a taste of that Lee fish." "I concur with my colleague." agreed Big M.

"Simmer down, boys. Play smart," said Bobbie Lee.

"Keep your heads on straight. Pay attention to orders," added Billie Rose. "Yes, team, just be cool. The Boss is on the way," I assured them.

It was now dark. The night light behind the store was not very bright, but I was fairly sure we would be able to identify anyone who might show up.

My phone rang again. "I'm three blocks away, but there has been a fender bender here that I'll need to check out until someone else gets here. I shouldn't be long," said Ross.

"I understand. All is quiet here."

I had hardly put my phone back in my pocket when a yellow van pulled up on the street beside the store. The driver just sat there, and then the door opened. I couldn't tell who it was when the light came on inside the cab, but a man moved slowly across the sidewalk and into the area behind the store.

The man was carrying a short ladder. He climbed the steps to the concrete dock along the back of the store. I could tell as he climbed that his feet were not in shoes. I could see fuzzy socks. They were red. I guessed he was disabling the alarm. Lee did say he had installed it, so I figured if it was him, it would not be a problem. He descended the ladder and knelt down by the lock.

"Steady, cats. Remember, observe, don't confront," I whispered.

I heard something click on the door. The door opened. Then I heard another click, and then another. Two cats took off. I grabbed my cell phone and quickly brought up Ross's number.

"He's here and the cats aren't taking orders," I said as I heard the Big voices of Moon Sun and Big M.

"STAY WHERE YOU ARE. DON'T MOVE!" growled the cats. "I'm on my way!" Ross shouted into the phone.

The man jumped up and headed for his van with Moon Sun and Big M in hot pursuit. He scrambled into the van and pulled out, nearly colliding with a passing car. He squealed out, burning rubber as his tires spun, gaining speed. Moon Sun and Big M headed back toward me. I was glad they, at least, didn't chase the van like a couple of silly dogs.

"He ran, Boss!" I shouted back.

I saw lights flashing as Ross flew by with his siren blazing.

F.A.T.C.A.T.

CHAPTER ELEVEN
SNOWFLAKE OR SHOW FAKE

"C.A.T., Load up!" I shouted.

"Hurry, Teddy, after him, I didn't get a bite," complained Moon Sun.

Big M scrambled into the basket, "Affirmative, he's a slippery scoundrel," he said.

"If you boys had paid attention to orders," Bobbie Lee said. "The boss probably would have gotten here in time to nab him."

Billie Rose agreed, "What part of 'observe, don't confront,' do you not understand, smarty britches." swatting Big M on the back of the helmet.

With all four felines on board, I got to the street and rode in the direction of Ross's pursuit. I could see his flashing lights in the distance. I guessed about six blocks. He must have pulled the van over in the church parking lot.

The area was appropriate because when I got there, I could hear the Boss preaching the gospel of you silly so-and-so, what are you trying to prove?

Ross held up his hand to caution me to keep a distance. I also kept a hand on the lid of the basket. The last thing we needed now was two crazy felines trying to take a bite out of red, fuzzy sock-covered ankles.

I could hear Ross's words. He said, "Elroy, you are being deceptive and dishonest. Don't you know that taking advantage of others is stealing? You're going to lose a lot more than you ever could have gained. How would you benefit if you gained the whole world, but lose your soul in the process? Think about it. I'm going to try to help you make up for what you've done. I know Max is gruff and mean, but remember, do unto others as you would have them do to you. Be a good example for Max. Change your ways, young man. You've got a lot of life ahead of you. You're going to meet a lot of bad people. You'll need help."

Ross put Elroy in his car. Then he came over, patted the lid of the basket and said, "Go to my house, Teddy. I'll be there in around an hour. I think we need to have a little talk with a couple of our team members. I don't think there will be a pizza party tonight."

"I understand, Ross. I'm sorry."

"It's not your fault, Teddy. We'll talk it out. Let's consider it a learning experience.

Felines could have gotten hurt, others could have gotten hurt. A chase situation is always dangerous. Hard telling what can happen. We need to know how serious our felines are. Do they want to make the F.A.T.C.A.T. work? If they want it to continue, this can't happen again. Take the cats home. You can go home if you want. I'll call you when I get back."

I felt bad. I understood how Moon Sun and Big M felt when they took off after Elroy, who they thought was Max. Maybe the big voice made them feel bigger and more powerful than they were. Something like Sam felt the first time he put on the football gear. He was angry. The gear made him feel powerful; more like lashing out. The cats developed a dislike for Max Lee and we dubbed him Lee Fish. They just wanted to go after him, and get a bite. They didn't think it through.

We arrived at Ross's house. I saw Mom had returned from her house-showing appointment, so I took off the cat's hats and told them I'd return when the Boss got home. They didn't have much to say. I think they understood that even though the lock bumper was caught, they'd let Ross down. They all went to their beds and curled up to wait.

When I walked in, Mom could tell there was a problem. She said, "You're earlier than I expected. What happened?"

"Good news and bad news," I answered. "Max Lee's assistant was breaking locks. He was trying to make things difficult for Max, perhaps frame him. We caught him, but he almost got away. Ross isn't very happy about how things went. We will be having a meeting when he gets home, and we won't be having a pizza celebration party."

"Not even pie and tuna cakes?" Mom asked. "I'm afraid not," I responded.

We talked a little more. It's an uncomfortable time when things don't go well and the boss is not happy. The phone rang.

"Come on over if you can, Teddy. We need to address this right now while everything is fresh on our minds," Ross said. "Also, let me talk to Tess before you hang up."

When I got there the cats were suited up with hats in place. They were on their stools around the table. Ross was pouring a cup of coffee. "Do you want something to sip on Teddy -- water, soft drink, hot chocolate?" he asked.

"No thanks," I answered.

I took a seat. Ross took a seat. He said, "My sweet, furry, lovable friends, don't you know I love you and couldn't bear it if anything bad happened to you?"

"Yes," "Yes," "Uh huh," "Yes, Boss," said four gloomy felines.

"Moon Sun, you take after your dad. You're fearless like him. He will cruise the neighborhood every night to see what's going on. He has no fear, but he is cautious, attentive, and watchful. These may be things you have yet to learn. You just do things without thinking about what could happen. Talk to me, tell me why I shouldn't hang up the helmets and scratch the F.A.T.C.A.T. project?" said a very concerned Ross.

Moon Sun straightened a bit and seemed to search for words, "Uh, well, I, uh, Boss I, I didn't like him! I was mad and not thinking clearly. I just wanted to get him, sorry. I let my feelings take over. I put my feelings ahead of your orders and what was best. I promise, I'll pay attention, I'll listen. Please don't quit on us, Boss. It won't happen again."

Ross broke in, "Enough, Moon Sun. I hope you're sincere. Now, the Midnight Marauder, M&M, Big M, my furry feline with the intellect of the professor you used to live with, you are much the same. However, you truly surprise me. You are very intelligent, usually think things through. What's your excuse for your careless actions? Talk to me!"

"It's true, Ross DuBoss, Master Detective, my genius owner and friend. I sit before you completely frustrated, totally confused about my behavior. It's not a simple matter, but I simply got caught up in the, to use Teddy's word, momentum, of the situation. I wanted so unreservedly to sink my teeth into that man. I apologize for my wrongful action and beseech your forgiveness," pleaded Big M.

Ross responded to his two pets' excuses, "Alright! You're not out of the woods. I've got some serious thinking to do. But, for now!" Ross threw his hands into the air ready to forgive and celebrate. "We did it again! High fives all around," Hands met paws, paws met paws, and paws met hands in high fives all around.

"I've talked to Tess, and understand that there is pie and tuna cake," announced Ross.

At that moment the doorbell rang and there was Mom with her fresh baked pie and tuna cakes.

"I brought ice cream for the apple pie," she said. "I want ice cream on my cake," said Moon Sun.

"How about a little ice cream on the side," I suggested.

Three crimes had been solved, criminals brought to justice with the help of the F.A.T.C.A.T., and now their crime fighting future was uncertain. But, for now we partied!

I awoke the next morning still feeling a bit troubled by the frustrating climax to the broken locks caper. I just hoped that Ross wouldn't choose to discontinue our experimental F.A.T.C.A.T. project. For now, however, I had other pressing matters on my mind. It was Wednesday. School would start next Thursday, and our first football game with the Zephyr Zebras was going to be a week from Friday. Why would anyone call themselves Zebras? Why not Wildcats, or Mountain Lions? Oh well, fact is, they are, at least have always been, a good football team, the one to beat. I wanted to do my part to make that happen. Today's practice and every practice for the next week would be very important. I tried to focus on football for now. It was difficult.

I decided not to ride my bike as I usually did. Jogging the ten or so blocks seemed a good idea. The sun was high enough in the sky that I could feel its warmth. The weather forecast for today and the whole week was mild. It would not be an unpleasant day to be in full gear. Maybe we'd scrimmage.

In the locker room I noticed Coach talking with our quarterback, Danny, with Sam standing by. I suited up and headed for the practice field.

Sam ran to catch up with me. From behind I heard, "Hey man, listen to this. Coach wants Danny to take me under his wing and give me some pointers. He wants me to be prepared to step in if Danny can't make it for some reason."

"Good deal," I responded. "I know you'd be great." "Yeah, but I'm not sure it's for me," offered Sam.

"Well, go along with it and see how it works out," I suggested. "Guess I'll have to," said Sam.

We reached the group of 32 boys, all ready to get with today's practice. After the warm-up, Coach divided us into the teams he wanted.

Danny, Sam, and I were going to practice offence. After about a dozen plays Coach pulled Danny aside. Then he called Sam over. He wanted him to run a few plays.

In the huddle Sam said, "Okay, guys, it's PR26. I need good blocking. Give me time to get a pass away."

It was a pass to the right side of the field to number 26, which was me.

"Okay, Teddy, run fast, get out there, let's make it a long one just like we did the other day when we were horsing around," said Sam. "Coach wants to see if that was for real."

Huddle broke and Sam slapped me on the back. Signals were called, the ball was hiked, and I was off like a flash. I ran thirty yards and looked back. Sam had already thrown the ball, and it was flying my way. It had just the right amount of lead. I raised my hands and there it was. It was almost like magic. I pulled the ball in and sprinted to the goal line. That day Coach found a perfect backup for Danny, maybe more.

As I jogged home, I replayed the pass reception. It was awesome. I thought how exciting that would be in a real game. Since I started organized football one of my dreams has been that my dad would be there to watch me. I imagined going out for the long pass with the score tied. I catch the ball and cross the goal line for the winning score, and my dad comes to his feet cheering for his son....

I shook my head to bring myself back to reality, and walked into Miss Leona's kitchen for lunch. She had finished painting another room.

"Help me move furniture back, Teddy, after lunch?" she asked. "You bet, be glad to. Why that color, Miss Leona?" I questioned.

I noticed she had painted it green while she had painted other rooms shades of brown. "I like it mainly," she answered. "I'll put the accessories together later to match the color. It's a guest bedroom. But, I really like that shade of green." "Okay, whatever you say. If you like it, I do too." I agreed.

Miss Leona gave me a big smile and asked, "Teddy, tonight is Midtown's annual feline competition. You like cats. Would you like to go? I think you'd enjoy it.

Your mom is free tonight and she thinks it would be fun. So what do you say? The reigning champion is Snowflake. Guess who she belongs to?"

"I have no idea," I said.

"Martha Edding, Chief Edding's wife. Sam's grandmother," she revealed.

It seemed like no time until Mom and I were on our way to Miss Leona's house ready to take in the big cat show. I love cats, but I had never seen a cat show, or competition.

It was interesting. The cats were inspected. They were posed in front of the judges.

Then the judges appeared to be in deep thought. They walked around the cats again. Then they huddled together to deliberate. The cats were put in their pet taxis where they waited out of the arena until the judges reached a decision.

Finally, the people showing were asked to go bring their cats back in so the winners could be announced. Third place was revealed. Then second, and finally first place was announced, "The winner of this year's Midtown Feline Competition is Snowflake, owned by Martha Edding."

I watched as Mrs. Edding brought her pet taxi to the winner's circle and removed Snowflake. I noticed he had a dirty toe as she set her in the place of honor. Suddenly, Mrs. Edding drew back from her cat and just stood there.

The judges asked her, "What's wrong Martha?"

CHAPTER TWELVE
BLACK TOE

Martha pointed to the right front foot. "This cat has black toes. That's not Snowflake. Snowflake is completely white. No other color anywhere. This cat is an imposter!"

My thoughts went immediately to – this is a job for the F.A.T.C.A.T.

There was much confusion in the arena among the judges and the other cat owners.

Everyone was asking, "How could this happen?"

Martha received her award as did the second and third place winners. The cat imposter was taken by the Midtown Animal Services for safe keeping until things could be sorted out.

Detective Ross DuBoss, special advisor to the MPD, showed up to investigate.

Detective Iverson and Chief Edding also appeared on the scene. Mom, Miss Leona, and I headed home.

Saturday's headline in the Midtown Messenger read:

Show Fake Switched with Snowflake Grand Champion of Midtown's Annual Cat Show

Police on the scene could not explain how or why the substitution was made. It is suspected that a ransom may be the motive. Snowflake is not only a past champion of the Midtown Cat Show, but the State competition as well. She is a valuable feline……………………....................................

The phone rang.

"Hello, Tesslemans. This is Teddy," I answered.

"Hey Teddy, Ross here. It's time to rally the troops. Come on over and we'll exchange views. We'll consider how to pursue this investigation. Chief Edding asked for our help. That's you and me. If he only knew how much help he was really getting."

I was happy that Ross was ready to continue with the F.A.T.C.A.T.

"I'll be right over," I said hanging up the phone.

Mom was expecting that the team would get together. She just said, "Keep in touch, Teddy. Let me know if you leave."

"Okay, we're going to have a powwow. Maybe come up with a plan. Talk to you later," I replied as I flew out the door.

I think all were talking at the same time when I saw Ross and the cats. I grabbed my headset, eager to hear all the chit chat.

"I'm ready to chew the case over," said Bobbie Lee.

"Let's not talk about chewing," said Billie Rose. "That's what got us in trouble." "Right, sorry." responded Bobbie Lee. "I mean talk it over."

"That's better. Maybe hash it out."

"Yes, let's deal with the missing Snowflake. The F.A.T.C.A.T. is going to have a bull session," offered Moon Sun.

"It is time to analyze the situation. Let us converse, have a big confabulation," said M&M.

Ross came back, "That's right, we are going to have a discussion. Here are the facts I've uncovered so far.

1. Obviously Snowflake was removed from the pet taxi and the imposter placed inside in her place.
2. There are only two ways into the holding room. One from the arena, one from the alley.
3. The door from the alley was locked when the competition began.
4. There was a half hour period of time when the exchange could have been made.

That was after the showing, when the judges were deliberating from 9:00 to 9:30. Anyone care to offer a suggestion, a strategy, a place to start?" asked Ross.

"Where are our petnappers?" asked Bobbie Lee.

"They're still in lock-up awaiting their trial," reported Ross.

Billie Rose asked, "Has Martha been in contact with anyone lately who might have anything to gain from taking Snowflake? And why exchange the show fake for Snowflake?"

"Good question," responded Ross.

"Who is this imposter anyway? Where did he come from? Should we see if my dad knows anything about a white cat with a black toe?" asked Moon Sun.

"Wouldn't hurt," agreed Ross. "It's getting late. Teddy, can you go with me tomorrow afternoon to talk to Martha? Then later we'll try to find Moon and see if he has any information on the imposter."

"Great! It's a start," I offered. "Yeah,"

"Right," "Exactly,"

"Affirmative," came four F.A.T.C.A.T. voices.

I let Mom know what we were up to, and listened to her feedback, then went to my room to think and rest.

I slept soundly. I had a dream of a big white cat with a black toe. It was so strange to be perfectly white except for one toe on his right front foot. In my dream the black- toed cat and Snowflake were running together in the darkness. Snowflake seemed very happy as they ran through the countryside.

It was Saturday. I had my usual Saturday activities. At lunch I met Ross and we went to talk to Martha.

"My house seems so empty without my cat," she cried. "I miss her every minute."

Ross patted her shoulder. "We'll find Snowflake. Has anyone taken an unusual interest in her lately? Have any strangers been around?" he asked.

Martha thought, then she responded, "I had a man paint my privacy fence last week, and then I had him clean out my garage. He was rather taken with Snowflake and Snowflake with him. I couldn't put her out back because I didn't want her to rub against the wet paint. The man petted her before he started. I usually let Snowflake wander around in the backyard a little every day. That's why I have the privacy fence. It is six feet high. I don't have to worry about her climbing it because she doesn't have claws, and it's too high for her to jump."

Ross asked, "Do you know where the painter lives?"

Martha answered, "I know him, his name is Arnie. He has an ad in the newspaper, and in the phone book. I'll show you."

"Have you heard from anyone about your cat?" asked Ross. "You realize whoever took her may want money for her return."

"I'm aware of that. The Chief is recording and tracing our phone calls, as you probably know, in the event that happens," said Martha, her voice shaking.

"Okay, thanks, Martha. Don't worry, It'll be alright," comforted Ross.

We found the painter's home, but didn't want to contact him quite yet. Perhaps surveillance was needed here? Right now we wanted to get the C.A.T. and see if we could find Moon Sun's dad, Moon.

At Ross's house, we suited up the team and headed out. The cats were eager to get out into the field, especially Moon Sun. He hadn't talked to his dad in a while.

When we opened the car door four eager cats took off. Ross and I just sat back and let them do the legwork. However, Moon wasn't hard to find. Once in the thicket where his father usually hung out, Moon Sun began to quiz him.

"Are you aware of a white cat with a black toe on his right front foot?"

With Moon Sun standing close to his dad, Moon's sounds were translated through Moon Sun's mic so Ross and I could understand what he was saying.

"Yes, I am. He comes through the thicket from time to time. He doesn't have a home. He just wanders around to all the food hand-out places. Why do you ask?"

"He is involved in our latest case. Any information you can give us about his whereabouts for the last day or so would be a big help," said Moon Sun.

Moon replied, "I haven't seen him in a while."

"That's because he's being held by Animal Services. He was found taking the place of Midtown's princess of cats, Snowflake. How he got there and where Snowflake has gone is our latest mystery," said Moon Sun. "Can you help us?"

Moon answered, "Check back with me in a day or so. I'll see what I can find out."

The C.A.T. ran back to the car. We headed home not knowing any more than before. However, we found out that Moon knew Black Toe. Now he was seeking information for us.

Ross said, "Tomorrow is Sunday. Our time is limited and I don't like pursuing a case on Sunday, but we don't want the trail to grow cold.

I suggested, "Why don't we check out the painter in the afternoon." "My thoughts exactly." agreed Ross.

Around 1 p.m. we parked in a business lot across the street from the painter's home.

We waited. We had left the cats at home. Four more sets of eyes might have been valuable, but sometimes those four little bodies can be distracting. Chances were they would have spent the time snoozing anyway.

After a short time we saw the painter, Arnie Doolittle, approaching his home. He was carrying a big bag of what appeared to be kitty litter. To us this looked suspicious. We left our vehicle to confront Arnie. I hoped his last name was no indication of his work. If it was, maybe he did need the money a ransom might bring.

By the time we got there he had entered his house. We knocked on the door. Arnie came to the door and asked, "Can I help you?"

"Mr. Doolittle, I'm detective Ross DuBoss. I'd like to ask you some questions about the cat you met when you were painting for Martha Edding."

At that moment we heard a meow. A beautiful tabby cat appeared. It was a gray- black mix with black blotches here and there. It rubbed against Arnie's leg and purred.

"Oh yes, yes, most certainly, I love cats and she is a real prize, a pure delight, almost as fine as my Caramel Joe here. I was getting ready to paint the fence. That's what I do, paint. I didn't spend much time with her, unfortunately."

Ross explained, "She's missing, Mr. Doolittle. Someone replaced her with an imposter at the Midtown Cat Show Friday evening."

"You don't say. How terrible, how shocking! Why would anyone do that?" he inquired as Caramel Joe, eager for attention, made figure eights around his legs. "I don't know how I can help you. I certainly didn't take her. What would my Caramel Joe think? I am perfectly content with my Joe boy here."

"You have already helped, Mr. Doolittle. We can eliminate you as a suspect. If you think of anything that might help us, please let us know."

Mr. Doolittle called out as we were leaving, "I did notice something when I went into the backyard before I started painting. Snowflake, that pretty girl, was outside. She seemed to be aware of someone or something on the other side of the fence. She pranced back and forth, bounced around looking at the fence. She even seemed to be looking through the spaces between the boards. And, when I was on the other side of the fence, I saw a big white cat that I thought was Snowflake. Mercy, Snowflake, how did you get over here you silly girl, I thought. The cat took off running into the woods beside their property. When I went to check with Mrs. Edding, Snowflake was in the house. I don't know if that is important, if it's helpful, but I do know there was another cat around that looked a lot like pretty Snowflake."

"Thank you, Arnie. You've been very helpful," said Ross.

"Very peculiar, don't you think?" I said to Ross as we walked back to the car. "Yes, very," agreed Ross. "Now it seems our biggest suspect is a big white cat with a black toe. How? Why? It makes no sense."

After we went home, I kept thinking about the case. A black-toed cat appears, the show champion disappears, the door was locked, and the pet taxi door was latched. That night I had cat dreams again.

Monday morning football practice went well. Sam practiced in the quarterback spot again. He made a half dozen pass plays, all of which were successful. If we didn't already have a good quarterback, Sam would be a shoo-in for the position. I was having a hard time thinking of school starting in three days and the big game on Friday. Snowflake kept controlling my thoughts. It reminded me of my dad. Suddenly he's gone for weeks, then months. *When will he return? Will Snowflake be like this too? Who is this cat that took her place? How did he get there?*

I was glad to see evening approaching. Soon we'd learn what Moon had found out about a certain black-toed cat.

With the C.A.T. in place and their transmitters on, Ross and I were tuned in to the information Moon had to share.

"Well, the story is, from the local strays and other cats wandering the neighborhood, that Black Toe was scheming to help Snowflake see the outside world," offered Moon.

"Very interesting, I guess we need to interrogate the black-toed cat," I said. "Right you are," agreed Ross. "I'll make arrangements to pick him up."

We drove by Animal Services and picked up Black Toe. I'm sure he didn't know what to think when we took him into Ross's house where he was surrounded by four weird-looking cats with hat/helmet/bonnets on.

The questioning began.

"What do you know about Snowflake?" "How did you end up in her pet taxi?" "Did someone switch you for her?"

"It is our ambition to ascertain the vicinity of her presence."

Black Toe shook his head looking a little bewildered and began to give information. He inched over beside me. I think he felt more comfortable there. "Perhaps I should begin at the beginning. A few days ago I was talking to Snowflake through her privacy fence. She informed me of her desire to see the outside world. She wished she could trade places with me. She told me that she was very lucky to be treated nice. People thought she looked good, so she was going to be in another contest. That gave me an idea. I figured if I could get into the room where she was being kept then maybe I'd have a chance to trade places with her. We look a lot alike other than I'm a boy and she's a girl and I have a black toe. I thought it might buy her enough time to get away for a while. It was worth a try. It worked. I slipped in the alley door when all the cats were being brought in. I hid out until the contest was over and just the cats were in the room. I jumped up on the table where Snowflake's cage was and slid the door catch over, opened the door, Snowflake came out, I went in, she shut the door and hid until the alley door was opened again. She slipped out and is out there exploring the world. I know she will return home soon once she's soothed her curiosity and gets hungry."

The words had hardly been translated when the phone rang. Martha was calling to tell Ross that she had just found Snowflake on her front porch. We knew what had happened. All Martha knew was her cat was home.

The Chief might listen to Ross and believe it, but Ross still wasn't ready to share our F.A.T.C.A.T. project. Maybe the best thing to do was just return Black Toe to Animal Services and let it go at that, which is what we did.

Ross didn't seem to mind. He even wanted to have a pizza party to celebrate our unofficial success.

"Hey, I'm always up for a pizza celebration," I agreed. "Let's have it at your house for a change," Ross requested. "Fine by me," I said.

"Would you pick up the F.A.T.C.A.T. after football practice tomorrow? We'll make it a lunch party. Don't put on their gear. I'll check with your mom and hopefully she'll join us. You can even invite Miss Leona. I'm bringing a special guest also and we'll celebrate."

After practice I removed the basket from my bike and loaded it with the cats. I carried the basket into my house, set it down, and opened the lid. When I looked up I saw a big white cat walk from the kitchen to the dining room.

"What is he doing here?" I asked.

Mom said, "Your answer is in the kitchen."

F.A.T.C.A.T.

CHAPTER THIRTEEN
PERFECT

I walked into the dining room where Mom and Miss Leona were standing. Hidden behind them was a big cake with thirteen candles on it. In the kitchen, there was a representative from the Midtown Animal Services.

He said, "Hello Teddy. Ross mentioned yesterday that if it is alright with your mom, you could give this cat a good home. It is your birthday. You've always wanted a cat, I'm told. How about it?"

I looked at Mom. She smiled and said, "I think it's about time, don't you? And, he needs a home. Happy birthday!"

"Really? What will Dad say when he gets home?"

"We'll worry about that when he gets home, dear. Things may be different then." "Okay, Mom! Cool, my very own cat. I hope he gets along with Ross's cats. I wonder if he likes anchovies? Let's eat."

I wondered if Mom was giving up on Dad making it back, or if she knew something she wasn't ready to share. Something didn't seem right here.

The man from Animal Services shook my hand. "Well alright then, Black Toe has a home, you have a cat, and I have a piece of pizza and birthday cake." And he left.

There were four, then there were five. They sat in a circle looking at each other making their sounds. I was wishing we all had on our gear so we knew what they were saying. The sounds were calm. All was well.

After lunch Ross and Mom went back to work. I walked over to Miss Leona's to help her with some stuff. I heard a splashing, pop, pop, sound as we entered her garden.

"What is that noise?" I asked.

"Noise, what noise? Really, Teddy, you call that soothing sound of water in my garden pool – noise?"

Then I noticed the fountain that sprayed into the air in her little pond. "Oh, you've got it going. That's neat, Miss Leona, and there's fish. How many?"

"There're four. They're small. Sometimes they hide, but they are all there somewhere."

Two of them were making the popping sound as they hit the surface of the water grabbing bits of food that Miss Leona must have sprinkled on the water before she came over for our celebration lunch and to see our new family member.

"Two things, Teddy. One – maybe Black Toe shouldn't meet my fish just yet. I saw how he devoured the anchovies. And two – I have pretty rocks and plants to place around the pond. What do you say? Do you want to help me decorate and fix it up nice?"

"Yeah, great! I like doing stuff like that. What's first?"

I enjoyed helping Miss Leona, Then I went home to start getting acquainted with Black Toe. I don't know how, but I could tell when I looked into his eyes that he was happy and intelligent. I wondered how he would adapt to a helmet. I couldn't wait to actually talk to him. I noticed when I was petting him and rubbing his paws that he didn't have claws, which indicated that he hadn't always been a homeless prowler. Questions were stacking up that I wanted to ask him. For now we just spent some quiet time together.

He was an unusual looking cat. I hadn't noticed, but he didn't just have a black toe, he also had the tiniest black tip on his tail. His fur wasn't real long. It was like Big M's, medium length. I'd have to brush him from time to time to keep him looking handsome. He got on my lap and stood up on his hind legs, put his front paws on my shoulders and nuzzled my face with his nose. He looked at me as if to say, "Thank you, Teddy!"

I didn't hear it, but I heard it. I know that doesn't make any sense. Maybe he was talking to me through his touch. Maybe he was sending me the words telepathically, I think that's what it's called, where you communicate with your mind. I don't know, but I heard it in my head. I was sure he was glad to have a home with me.

I looked at Black Toe straight in the eyes and said, "You're a cool cat, I'm really glad you're going to be my cat. I've wanted you my whole life. Now here you are." He was more than the cat of my dreams. He was my newest friend.

Wednesday morning as I jogged to practice I thought how the summer had been one to remember. F.A.T.C.A.T. had gotten off to a successful start. We apprehended a jewel thief, petnappers, and a lock bumper, and then solved the mystery of the cat-show fake. I'd been promoted in the Junior Detective Program. I made the Junior High School football team as a running back. I was building a friendship with Sam. Miss Leona had come into our lives and had given Mom peace of mind. Now the big game was only two days away. Only two things could make the summer any better.

One – we beat the Zebras, two – my dad would be there to watch my first game. I had doubts on both counts. I knew I was going to do everything I could to beat the Zebras, but I had no control over my dad's whereabouts. I could just dream and pray.

Practice was tough. We went through every play in the playbook at least twice.

Everyone was saying, "Coach, have a heart."

Finally he motioned for all of us to gather around. "In two days you'll play your first game of the season. It could be the one that matters most. You have been attending summer practice for a month. We have some great talent. The Zephyr Zebras usually beat the Midtown Wizards, but you can change that. I think you will, but it's up to you now."

That evening Ross and I began working on Black Toe's helmet. He sat calmly watching as we cut the leather and embedded the technology needed to make it work. Then we stuck it together with adhesive and stitches. It reminded me of the old leather football helmets players wore many years ago. Sam and I saw one on the wall of the Active Life Buffet and Grill. Our cats are part of a team, but the helmets are not to protect. They are made to let us communicate, and they do.

"Let's try it on for size before we go any farther, Ross," I suggested.

"Yes," Ross agreed. "Get Moon Sun. Put his helmet on, and we'll have him explain to Black Toe what we're doing. We don't want him to get spooked when we try it on."

Moon Sun helped us out. We put the helmet on Black Toe. It fit.

"In a day or two, when it's finished, we'll teach him how to use it," Ross said.

I went home thinking, Tomorrow school begins. Day after is the big game. When I walked into the house, Mom was just hanging up the phone. She looked like she had just won a prize or something.

"What's up, Mom?

"Oh, nothing," she said, wrapping her arms around herself and spinning around like a schoolgirl who had just gotten her first date.

"I think you're up to something, Mom."

"No I'm not," she said batting her eyes and acting like a kid again.

I wondered why she was so goofy. Had she made a big real estate deal? Surely if she had, she would share it with me. It was soon going to be my birthday. Was she planning a surprise party? Every time I saw Mom the next two days she was giddy and silly. Something was up, but she wasn't telling.

School was okay Thursday. I had a hard time Friday. The game was upon us. Ordinarily junior high games were played earlier in the week, but the high school's first game was going to be the second week of school. So, we were opening the season tonight – Friday.

The game was to start at 6:00p.m. I was in the locker room at 5:00. We were on the practice field at 5:30, warming up. At 5:45 we ran out on the game field to the cheers of a nice crowd. I looked toward the bleachers searching for familiar faces. I saw Mom, Miss Leona, Lois, Ross, Chief Edding, but, no, I didn't see the face of the person I had dreamed of being there, my dad. I was disappointed, but not surprised. It wasn't realistic to think he might miraculously appear. That would be too good to be true.

Coach gathered us around. "Okay, guys. You've worked hard. You're ready. Go do it!

The Zebras are going down!"

The Zebras won the toss and chose to receive. The ball was kicked and the game began. Four plays later the Zebras scored and got the extra point. The score after about 10 minutes on the field was 7 to 0, Zebras.

It was our turn. Strangely, believe it or not, four plays later, we scored and got the extra point. At the end of the first quarter the score was tied. There was no score in the second quarter. Half-time found the score still tied.

I looked at the bleachers. The same people were still there. Mom waved when she saw me looking. So did the rest of our group.

The second half started. In the third quarter the Zebras scored again. They failed to get the extra point. Now the score was 13 to 7, Zebras. The last quarter began. We played hard. Neither team scored any points. Then, Danny got tackled hard. He twisted his ankle.

Coach called a time-out. "Sam, help us out, we need you. What do you say?" "Sure, Coach, we'll just go out there and win this thing. We'll do it for Danny."

The game resumed. A couple of plays moved the ball into Zebra territory. The time was running out.

Sam called the play, "Okay guys, It's PR26. You block. I throw. Teddy catches. We win. Easy as that."

I looked at the bleachers. Someone else had joined the group. Couldn't focus right now. Had a pass to catch. The ball was hiked, Sam moved around in the pocket. I moved fast down field. Just like a few times before, I looked up and there came the ball, like magic. It fell into my hands and I sprinted across the goal line. I could hear the cheers from the crowd. As I turned and threw the ball down like big guy players do the buzzer sounded.

The extra point was good. The Midtown Wizards had beaten the Zephyr Zebras.

Kids were jumping up and down. Adults were hugging and yelling praises to us. People were coming out on the field. My teammates were lifting Sam and me up on their shoulders to parade us around. In the midst of this, the person who had joined Mom and the others was headed my way.

"Dad? Dad!" I screamed as I struggled to get down off shoulders and on my own two feet. I ran to him, tears streaming down my face. He fell to his knees with his arms wide open for an embrace into which I collapsed.

Holding me he said, "I've missed you so much, son. What a game. I'm proud of you, Teddy."

Stepping back I saw tears rolling down his face as well. I just looked at the face I hadn't seen for nearly a year. I could not take my eyes off him. How great it would be for him to see more of my games. How wonderful it would be with my mom and dad and me together again. I had so many questions, but they could wait until later when we were home. It was perfect, perfect, this day was perfect. My other dream had come true. My dad was home and he had seen me play in my first organized football game. And he saw us win.

Ross, Mom, and Miss Leona had joined us. They were patting me on the back and congratulating me. I smiled at them and headed for the locker room to hear the coaches wrap-up, get rid of the pads and get dressed. My head was spinning. Questions, questions, did I ever have questions. But, not just questions. There was so much to tell Dad.

F.A.T.C.A.T., would he be surprised, shocked might be a better word. Then, the piano duet Mom and I had prepared. I couldn't wait to get home. My dad, and my new friend, Black

Toe, would be there. How was this going to work? Mom had said that things would be different. What did she mean? I didn't know, but this I did know. Things have a way of working out. God is good. Prayers are answered.

F.A.T.C.A.T.

By
David D. Felty
Scripture References
NIT

Lightning Source UK Ltd.
Milton Keynes UK
UKHW022242171120
373592UK00003B/280